Prepared in cooperation with the U.S. Army Corps of Engineers

Simulating Potential Structural and Operational Changes for Detroit Dam on the North Santiam River, Oregon— Interim Results

By Norman L. Buccola and Stewart A. Rounds

Open-File Report 2011–1268

U.S. Department of the Interior
U.S. Geological Survey

U.S. Department of the Interior
KEN SALAZAR, Secretary

U.S. Geological Survey
Marcia K. McNutt, Director

U.S. Geological Survey, Reston, Virginia 2011

For product and ordering information:
World Wide Web: http://www.usgs.gov/pubprod
Telephone: 1-888-ASK-USGS

For more information on the USGS—the Federal source for science about the Earth,
its natural and living resources, natural hazards, and the environment:
World Wide Web: http://www.usgs.gov
Telephone: 1-888-ASK-USGS

Contents

Figures

Tables

Conversion Factors and Datums

Multiply	By	To obtain
foot (ft)	0.3048	meter (m)
mile (mi)	1.609	kilometer (km)
acre-foot (acre-ft)	1,233	cubic meter (m^3)
foot per second (ft/s)	0.3048	meter per second (m/s)

Temperature in degrees Celsius (°C) may be converted to degrees Fahrenheit (°F) as follows:
°F=(1.8×°C)+32

Temperature in degrees Fahrenheit (°F) may be converted to degrees Celsius (°C) as follows:
°C=(°F-32)/1.8

Vertical coordinate information is referenced to the North American Vertical Datum of 1988 (NAVD 88).

Horizontal coordinate information is referenced to the North American Datum of 1983 (NAD 83).

Elevation, as used in this report, refers to distance above the vertical datum.

Simulating Potential Structural and Operational Changes for Detroit Dam on the North Santiam River, Oregon—Interim Results

By Norman L. Buccola and Stewart A. Rounds

Executive Summary

Prior to operational changes in 2007, Detroit Dam on the North Santiam River in western Oregon had a well-documented effect on downstream water temperature that was problematic for endangered salmonid fish species. In this U.S. Geological Survey study, done in cooperation with the U.S. Army Corps of Engineers, an existing calibrated CE-QUAL-W2 model of Detroit Lake (the impounded waterbody behind Detroit Dam) was used to determine how changes in dam operation or changes to the structural release points of Detroit Dam might affect downstream water temperatures under a range of historical hydrologic and meteorological conditions.

Many combinations of environmental, operational, and structural options were explored with the model. Two downstream temperature targets were used along with three sets of environmental forcing conditions representing normal, hot/dry, and cool/wet conditions. Three structural options were modeled, including the use of existing outlets, one hypothetical variable-elevation outlet such as a sliding gate, and a hypothetical combination of a floating outlet and a fixed-elevation outlet. Finally, four sets of operational guidelines were explored to gain an understanding of the effects of imposing different downstream minimum streamflows or managing the level of the lake with different timelines in autumn.

Several conclusions can be made from these interim model scenarios:

- Temperature targets just downstream of Detroit Dam can be met through a combination of new dam outlets or a delayed drawdown of the lake in autumn.

- Spring and summer dam operations greatly affect the available release temperatures and operational flexibility later in the autumn. Releasing warm water during mid-summer tends to keep more cool water available for release in autumn.

- The ability to meet downstream temperature targets during spring depends on the characteristics of the available outlets. Under existing conditions, for example, although warm water sometimes is present at the lake surface, such water may not be available for release if the lake level is either well below or well above the spillway crest in spring and early summer.

- Managing lake releases to meet downstream temperature targets depends on having outlet structures that can access both (warm) lake surface water and (cold) deeper lake water throughout the year. The existing outlets at Detroit Dam do not allow near-surface waters to be released during times when the lake surface level is below the spillway (spring and autumn).

- Model simulations indicate that delayed drawdown of Detroit Lake in autumn would result in better control over release temperatures.

- Compared to the existing outlets at Detroit Dam, floating or sliding-gate outlet structures can provide greater control over release temperatures because they provide better access to warm water at the lake surface and cooler water at depth.

This report provides interim study results to the U.S. Army Corps of Engineers. The full study will be completed in 2012.

Background

Detroit Lake is a man-made reservoir impounded by Detroit Dam on the North Santiam River in western Oregon (fig. 1). The North Santiam River drains an area on the western slopes of the Cascade Range, and is one of several major tributaries to the Willamette River. Detroit Dam is the tallest dam (463 ft) in the Willamette River basin and impounds 455,100 acre-feet of water at full pool, making it also one of the largest reservoirs in the basin. The Big Cliff–Detroit Dam complex typically generates more hydroelectric power than any other U.S. Army Corps of Engineers (USACE) facility in the Willamette River basin, and Detroit Lake ranks as one of the most important recreational resources among the 13 reservoirs managed by USACE in the Willamette Project.

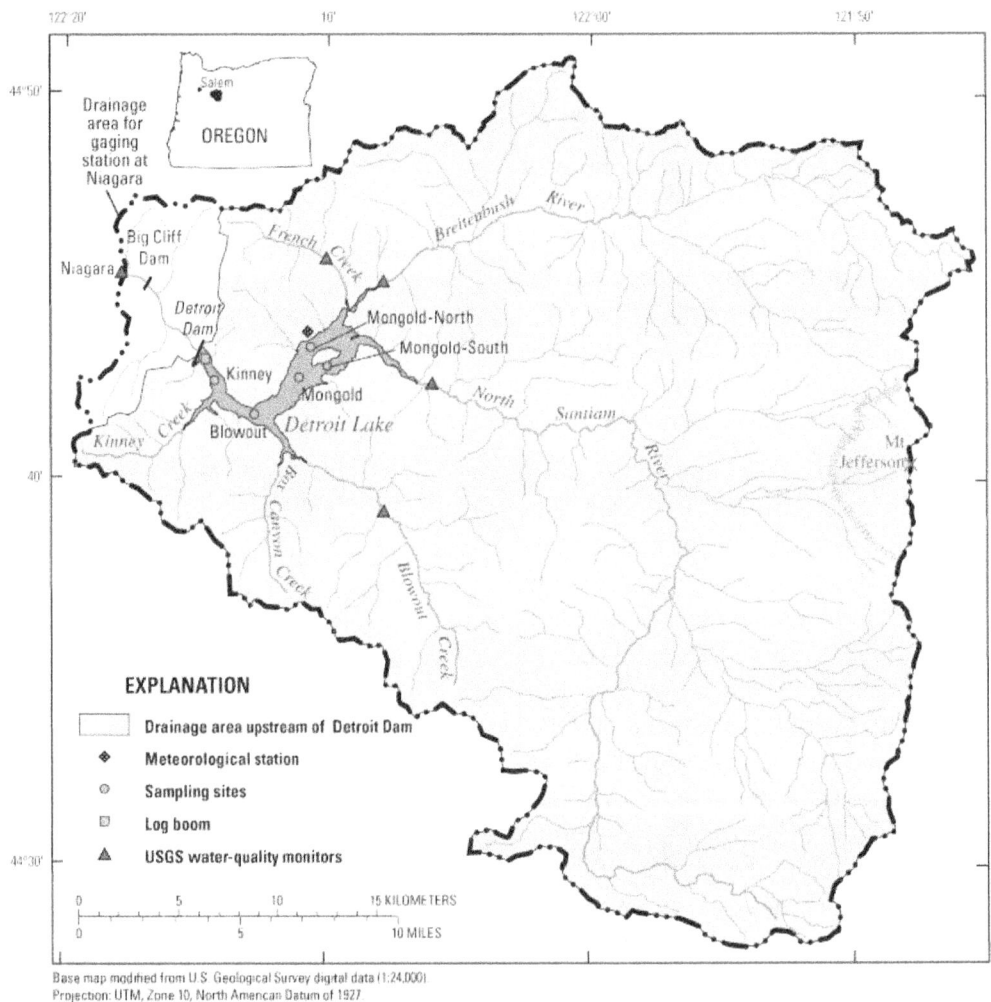

Figure 1. Map showing the location of Detroit Lake, Detroit Dam, and Big Cliff Dam in the North Santiam River basin in western Oregon (map reproduced from Sullivan and others, 2007).

The U.S. Geological Survey (USGS) constructed a model of Detroit Lake to examine water temperature and suspended sediment conditions in the lake and downstream (Sullivan and others, 2007). The model was built using CE-QUAL-W2, a two-dimensional, laterally averaged flow and water-quality model from the USACE (Cole and Wells, 2002). The USGS model was calibrated to conditions that occurred during calendar years 2002 and 2003 and also tested for some high-flow conditions in 2006. The model is available online at *http://or.water.usgs.gov/santiam/detroit_lake/*.

The USGS model of Detroit Lake includes a custom subroutine that allows a model user to easily estimate release rates from different dam outlets that are necessary to achieve a time series of downstream temperature targets. In this way, dam operations can be forecasted in order to meet certain downstream fish habitat criteria at different times of the year.

Before 2007, power generation was a high priority for the Big Cliff–Detroit Dam complex, and releases from Detroit Dam generally were routed through the power penstocks except for times when excess flows were released through the upper regulating outlets (RO) or over the spillway. Since 2007, USACE has been operating the dam complex to manage downstream temperatures to meet the needs of high-value salmonid fish species, while at the same time balancing the need to generate hydropower. To better inform structural and operational planning decisions related to Detroit Dam outflow temperature management, the USACE asked the USGS to assist in temperature modeling of the Detroit Lake–Big Cliff Reservoir–North Santiam River system.

Purpose and Scope

The objective of this study is to use previously calibrated models of Detroit Lake and downstream waterbodies to determine the effects of potential operational and structural changes to Detroit Dam on downstream water temperatures. Working closely with USACE staff, USGS hydrologists have run a large number of model scenarios that include three different sets of environmental forcing conditions (*normal*, *hot/dry*, and *cool/wet*) superimposed on three different combinations of existing and hypothetical dam outlets, four possible operating schemes for flow releases and lake-level management, and two sets of downstream temperature targets.

This report documents results from the most important model scenarios as they stand on this date (September 2011) and describes the most important management factors (storage, dam operations), structural options, and environmental conditions (flow, weather) that determine the temperatures released from Detroit Dam. All results in this report are valid as of the date of its release, but could change and be superseded by findings later in the study.

Methods

Environmental Forcing Conditions

Three distinctly different environmental forcing scenarios were developed to evaluate temperature management operations and structural options at Detroit Dam in order to encompass a wide range of possible hydrologic and meteorological conditions in the North Santiam River basin. To ensure that the streamflow, water temperature, and meteorological datasets used to drive the models were consistent with one another, the simplest approach was to use historical datasets that represented a wide range of possible conditions, from cold and wet to normal to warm and dry.

This analysis is based primarily on the assumption that streamflow, along with meteorological conditions, is one of the most important factors influencing stream temperatures in Detroit Lake, Big Cliff Reservoir, and the North Santiam River. In many years, above-average streamflow (driven by snowmelt) during April–June can translate into above-average streamflow during July–September; therefore, the timing of runoff from snowmelt and precipitation may affect mid-summer temperatures, and the development of these environmental forcing scenarios must take that into account.

Because streamflow and temperature typically have less variability in late summer (August–September) prior to the autumn rainy season, and because years with a wet winter and spring do not necessarily have a wet autumn, the data were divided and analyzed in two time periods: winter–summer (January–September) and autumn (October–December). Dividing the year at the beginning of October not only made it easier to splice and transition model input data from separate years, but also resulted in an autumn wet season that is minimally dependent on the snowpack from the preceding winter and spring.

To choose scenarios with the most realistic range of streamflow and water temperature throughout the year, a method was devised to rank the 10 most recent years in which adequate data were available, using monthly mean streamflow and temperature data from the North Santiam River below Boulder Creek site upstream of Detroit Lake (USGS site 14178000). In order to avoid a high-flow bias in the monthly flow comparisons, the monthly streamflow was log-transformed prior to computing a difference between each month's flow and the long-term monthly median streamflow. This method allows the low-flow months to be compared more equally with high-flow months, and the differences between years can be assessed more clearly. To rank a group of months in each year, the sum of the differences between the log-transformed monthly mean streamflow and the log-transformed median of the monthly mean streamflow over the period of record (1929–2009) was computed and compared for the years 2000–2009.

Results for the January–September and October–December time frames are in table 1. The same procedure was applied to stream temperature data from the same site using a period of record of 1975–2009. This ranking procedure was used to guide further exploration of the hydrologic conditions that occurred in each year.

Table 1. Ranking of streamflow and water-temperature conditions at USGS site 14178000 (North Santiam River below Boulder Creek, Oregon) for two periods in each calendar year, 2000–2009.

[Ranks were calculated as log(monthly mean streamflow)–log(median monthly streamflow over entire period of record) and log(monthly mean temperature)–log(median monthly temperature over entire period of record). Colors indicate months that were concatenated for three scenarios: *normal*=green, *hot/dry*=brown, and *cool/wet*=blue.]

| Year | January–September | | October–December | |
	Streamflow	Temperature	Streamflow	Temperature
2000	7	4	2	2
2001	1	8	7	9.5
2002	9	3	1	6
2003	5	10	3	7
2004	4	9	4	9.5
2005	2	7	8	5
2006	6	5	10	8
2007	3	6	9	4
2008	10	1	5	3
2009	8	2	6	1

The rankings in table 1 and a visual comparison of the monthly data were used to develop three scenarios representing normal, dry, and wet conditions based primarily on rankings relating to streamflow. For example, the *normal* scenario was created by concatenating data from January–September of 2006 with data from October–December of 2009. Streamflow and stream temperature during the three chosen scenarios *(normal, hot/dry,* and *cool/wet)* are shown in figures 2 and 3. Because a large amount of variation in streamflow historically occurs during January–September, the three winter–summer scenarios were differentiated primarily by the quantity of streamflow occurring during the spring snowmelt period.

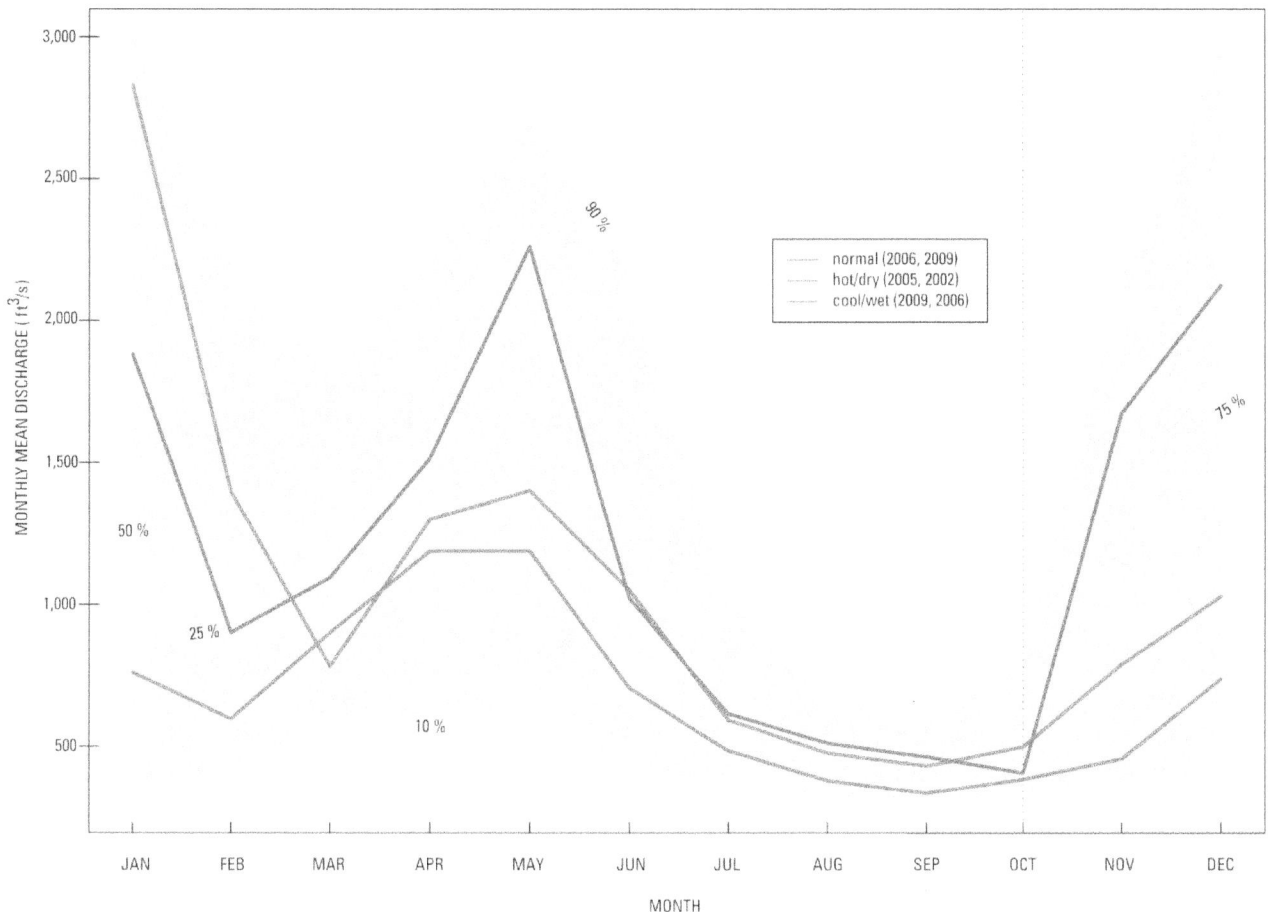

Figure 2. Monthly mean streamflow in the North Santiam River below Boulder Creek (USGS station 14178000) under three scenarios: *normal, hot/dry,* and *cool/wet.* The calendar years in the explanation parentheses denote the 2 years from which data were drawn and concatenated from the January–September and October–December periods. The 10th, 25th, 50th, 75th, and 90th percentiles (%) of the entire dataset from 1929–2009 are included for comparison.

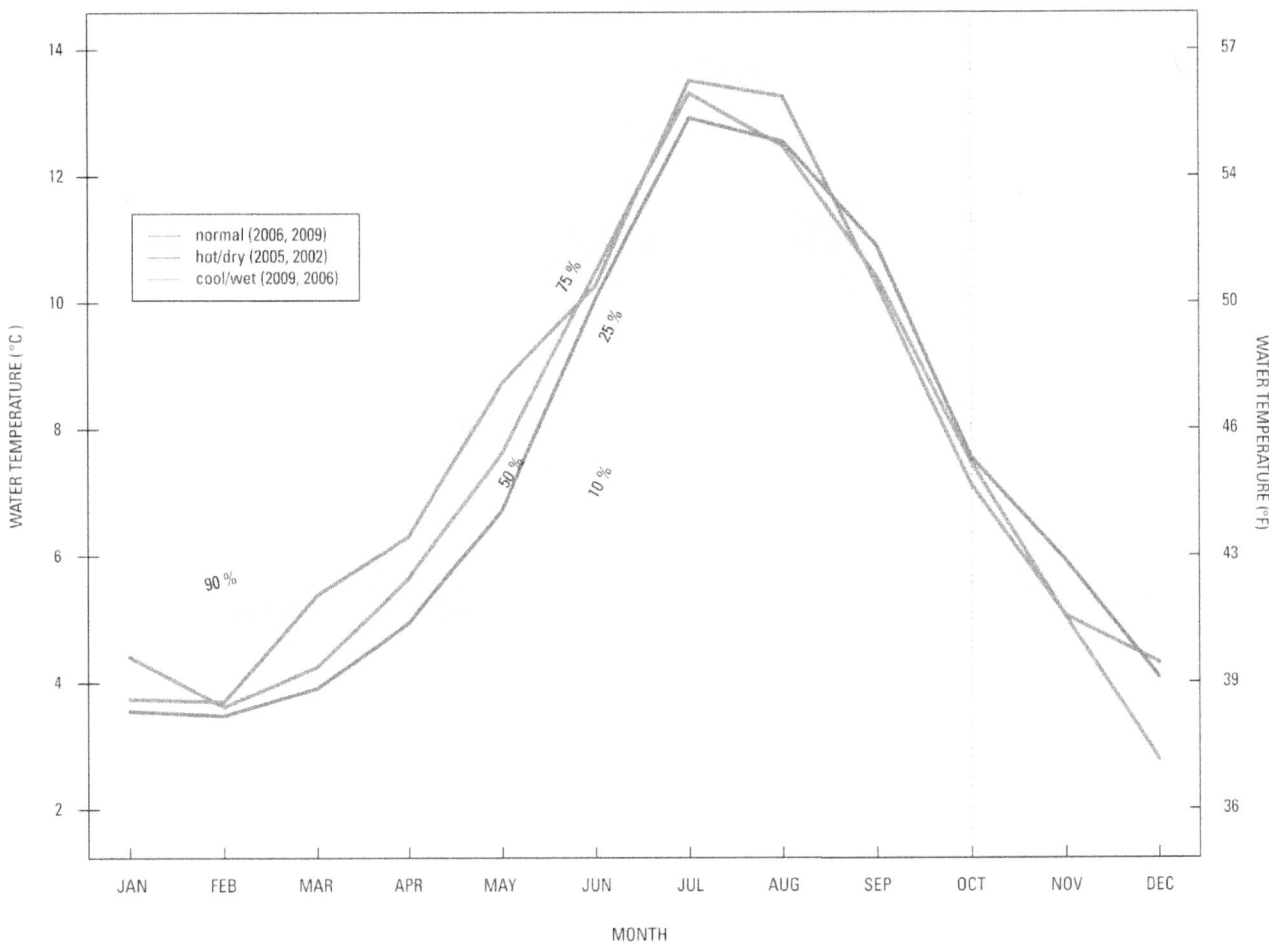

Figure 3. Monthly mean stream temperature in the North Santiam River below Boulder Creek (USGS site 14178000) under three scenarios: *normal, dry*, and *wet*. The years in the legend parentheses denote the 2 years from which data were drawn and concatenated from the January–September and October–December periods. The 10th, 25th, 50th, 75th, and 90th percentiles (%) of the entire dataset from 1975–2009 are included for comparison.

Together, the three environmental forcing scenarios span more than the 25th–75th percentiles of the historical data and do not exceed the 10th or 90th percentiles of streamflow and temperature. These environmental scenarios, therefore, encompass much of the typical variability in streamflow and water temperature, but without including rare and extreme hydrologic conditions. Most importantly, the *normal* scenario is very near the median for much of the year aside from January, March, and December.

Streamflow under the *hot/dry* scenario is very near the 25th percentile for the entire year, whereas monthly mean stream temperature is above the median for the year except for October

and November. The result is a "warm and dry" scenario.

Aside from February and October, monthly mean streamflow under the *cool/wet* scenario is above the median for the entire year. Interestingly, the extremely high flows occurring during autumn of the *cool/wet* scenario correspond to above average stream temperatures (probably owing to direct rainfall-runoff), whereas the high flows occurring earlier in the year produced below average stream temperatures (probably due to snowmelt). These results confirm the dependence of North Santiam River stream temperatures on snowmelt from the Cascade Range. Farther downstream, however, river temperatures will

6

depend greatly on dam operations and meteorological conditions.

Blending Algorithm and Temperature Targets

The custom blending algorithm within CE-QUAL-W2 v3.1, previously developed by USGS (Rounds and Sullivan, 2006; Sullivan and Rounds, 2006; Sullivan and others, 2007) was used in this study. This algorithm allows the model to blend releases using two outlets at a time and optimize a mixture of warmer water near the surface of the lake with cooler water from deeper in the lake in an attempt to match a user-specified time series of downstream temperature targets. The blending algorithm allows the user to specify several types of outlets, including floating, sliding-gate, and fixed-elevation outlet structures. Temperature targets that were previously developed and used by USACE on the McKenzie River system were applied to this study. Because these temperature targets include a minimum and maximum monthly value for much of the calendar year, those minima and maxima were used in separate model runs to establish a range in results.

For the scenarios described in this report, the custom blending algorithm in CE-QUAL-W2 was further modified and improved in several ways. First, the user now can specify that a minimum fraction of the total releases is assigned to a particular outlet. This allows, for example, the user to specify that at least 40 percent of the releases from Detroit Dam go through the powerhouse to generate electric power. That capability was used in several of the scenarios. Second, the user can specify a priority ranking for each of the outlets in an outlet group, such that one outlet is preferred for releases when the lake is isothermal and the choice of outlet has little to no effect on release temperatures. Again, this allows the user to assign more flow to power generation, for example, when the lake is isothermal. Finally, the blending algorithm itself was improved, incorporating an iterative solution method that greatly improved its ability to match the user-specified temperature target. Because the release temperature from each outlet is a function of flow, an iterative process is required to find the best combination of flows from two different outlets to match the user-specified temperature target.

Operational and Structural Scenarios

Based on potential future operational strategies and structural retrofit possibilities at Detroit Dam as assessed by USACE staff, model scenarios were devised to evaluate and compare the range of potential water temperatures that would likely exist downstream of Detroit Dam. Selected operational and structural scenarios then were projected onto the three environmental forcing conditions of *hot/dry*, *normal*, and *cool/wet* as well as both a minimum (*min*) and maximum (*max*) temperature target requirement. The temperature targets were established originally for the McKenzie River downstream of Cougar Dam, in the southern Willamette Valley, but now are being used for the North Santiam River downstream of Detroit Lake and Big Cliff Reservoir in the North Santiam River basin (table 2).

Table 2. Scenario group descriptions for the operational model for Detroit Dam on the North Santiam River, Oregon.

[RO, regulating outlet]

Temperature target	Environmental forcings	Structural scenarios	Operational scenarios
min	*cool/wet*	*existing*	*biop*
McKenzie River temperature target minimum	January–September 2009; October–December 2006	Existing outlets (spillway, power penstocks, and upper RO gates)	Existing operational rules following Biological Opinion minimum flow requirements
max	*normal*	*slider1340*	*spill_ext*
McKenzie River temperature target maximum	January–September 2006; October–December 2009	One sliding outlet from 1,340 ft elevation to the surface	Decreased minimum flow requirements during the summer
	hot/dry	*1340floater*	*spill_ext30*
	January–September 2005; October–December 2002	One floating outlet + one fixed outlet at 1,340 ft	Decreased minimum flow requirements during the summer; delayed drawdown by 30 days
			spill_ext45
			Decreased minimum flow requirements during the summer; delayed drawdown by 45 days

Hypothetical dam operational scenarios (*spill_ext*, *spill_ext_30*, and *spill_ext_45* scenario groups in tables 2 and 3) were imposed to evaluate the effects of delaying drawdown in the lake later in the autumn in three different ways.

To delay the drawdown of Detroit Lake, summer minimum releases from Detroit Dam as specified by the Biological Opinion (National Marine Fisheries Service, 2008) had to be decreased (table 3).

Table 3. Minimum and maximum flows for existing and hypothetical dam operational scenarios for Detroit Dam on the North Santiam River, Oregon

[Flows are daily mean streamflow, in cubic feet per second (ft^3/s). Numbers in italics indicate altered flows.]

Month and day	Existing flow requirements at Big Cliff Dam (*biop* scenario)	Altered flow requirements (*spill_ext*, *spill_ext_30*, and *spill ext 45* scenario groups)
	Minimum Flow (ft^3/s)	
January 1	1,200	1,200
February 1	1,000	1,000
March 1	1,000	1,000
March 16	1,500	1,500
April 1	1,500	1,500
May 1	1,580	*880*
May 16	1,580	*880*
June 1	1,280	*880*
July 1	1,280	*880*
July 16	1,080	*880*

Table 3. Minimum and maximum flows for existing and hypothetical dam operational scenarios for Detroit Dam on the North Santiam River, Oregon–continued

[Flows are daily mean streamflow, in cubic feet per second (ft^3/s). Numbers in italics indicate altered flows.]

Month and day	Existing flow requirements at Big Cliff Dam (*biop* scenario)	Altered flow requirements (*spill_ext, spill_ext_30,* and *spill_ext_45* scenario groups)
	Minimum Flow (ft³/s) (continued)	
September 1	1,500	*880*
October 16	1,200	1,200
December 1	1,200	1,200
December 31	1,200	1,200
	Maximum Flow (ft³/s)	
January 1		*15,000*
September 1	3,000	3,000
September 30	3,000	3,000
December 31		*15,000*

Structural scenarios were limited only by the three possible types of outlets that are available in the CE-QUAL-W2 v3.1 blending routine: fixed-elevation, floating, or sliding-gate. Both fixed-elevation and sliding-gate outlets have user-specified vertical limits in the depth of the lake while floating outlets have a user-defined depth at which the outlet floats below the surface. For this study, a lower limit of 1,340 ft (the elevation of the upper RO) and an upper limit of 6.6 ft (2 m) below the lake surface were specified for all floating and sliding-gate outlets. Three possible combinations of fixed-elevation, floating, and sliding-gate outlets were used in separate groups of structural scenarios and are specified in table 4.

Table 4. Summary and specification of model scenarios for the operation of Detroit Dam on the North Santiam River, Oregon

Environmental forcings	Temperature target	Structural scenarios	Operational scenarios	Scenario ID
cool/wet	*min*	*existing*	*biop*	*cmin1*
			spill_ext	*cmin2*
			spill_ext_30	*cmin3*
			spill_ext_45	*cmin4*
		slider1340	*biop*	*cmin5*
		1340floater	*biop*	*cmin6*
			spill_ext_30	*cmin7*
	max	*existing*	*biop*	*cmax1*
			spill_ext	*cmax2*
			spill_ext_30	*cmax3*
			spill_ext_45	*cmax4*
		slider1340	*biop*	*cmax5*
		1340floater	*biop*	*cmax6*
			spill_ext_30	*cmax7*

Table 4. Summary and specification of model scenarios for the operation of Detroit Dam on the North Santiam River, Oregon—continued

Environmental forcings	Temperature target	Structural scenarios	Operational scenarios	Scenario ID
normal	min	existing	biop	nmin1
			spill_ext	nmin2
			spill_ext_30	nmin3
			spill_ext_45	nmin4
		slider1340	biop	nmin5
		1340floater	biop	nmin6
			spill_ext_30	nmin7
	max	existing	biop	nmax1
			spill_ext	nmax2
			spill_ext_30	nmax3
			spill_ext_45	nmax4
		slider1340	biop	nmax5
		1340floater	biop	nmax6
			spill_ext_30	nmax7
hot/dry	min	existing	biop	hmin1
			spill_ext	hmin2
			spill_ext_30	hmin3
			spill_ext_45	hmin4
		slider1340	biop	hmin5
		1340floater	biop	hmin6
			spill_ext_30	hmin7
	max	existing	biop	hmax1
			spill_ext	hmax2
			spill_ext_30	hmax3
			spill_ext_45	hmax4
		slider1340	biop	hmax5
		1340floater	biop	hmax6
			spill_ext_30	hmax7

Model Setup and Use

Before running the model to simulate operational and structural scenarios at Detroit Dam, the previously developed USGS Detroit Lake model was set up and its calibration checked using measured inflows, outflows, and weather conditions from January 1 to August 30 in each environmental scenario. The only adjustment to model parameters was a minor change to the wind-sheltering coefficients to reflect the use of wind data from a station other than the one used for the original calibration.

After the model was configured, the difference between measured and modeled forebay elevations in the lake under each environmental scenario was used to determine the quantity of ungaged inflows and outflows for the lake, and an additional model input known as the distributed tributary was created for the model. This distributed tributary accounts for any unmeasured overland flows, evaporation, or groundwater flux not accounted for by other boundary conditions and serves to balance the water budget for the lake. A proportion of the inflow from each tributary was used to estimate the magnitude of the distributed tributary from September 1 to December 31 of each environmental scenario.

Following this water balance calibration, the total release rates (outflows) from Detroit Dam were computed by ensuring that the following conditions were met:

1. Minimum and maximum flow requirements (table 3)

2. The computed water level in Detroit Lake must not exceed the reservoir fill curve for more than 5 days.

3. Power peaking (use of the power penstock outlets) was assumed to occur during 0500–1200 and 1400–2200 each day*

*In reality, power peaking pertains only to the power penstock outlets; however, for simplicity in blending outflows within CE-QUAL-W2, all outlets were placed on this

flow schedule and used concurrently. Furthermore, power peaking was put in place only on days in which the daily average release rate was less than 2,472 ft³/s (70 m³/s). This rule helped ease the water balance of the downstream Big Cliff Reservoir model and comes closer to the way in which Detroit Dam is operated during large storm events.

For the *existing* structural scenario group (use of existing outlets), the computed total release rate was distributed among the available outlets. During times in which the forebay elevation in Detroit Lake was computed to be above the spillway, the total outflow was routed to the spillway and power penstocks, a combination that allows access to warm water near the lake surface (spillway) and cooler water at depth (power penstocks), thus achieving a blend of releases that is best positioned to meet the specified temperature target. When the elevation in the lake was computed to fall below the spillway crest, the only available outlets at Detroit Dam were the power penstocks and the upper ROs. The lower ROs are located below the power penstocks and upper ROs, but usage of those outlets may not be possible and was not assessed in this study. Under the *biop* operational scenario group, the rules for dam releases that are currently in use by USACE were applied to each environmental scenario.

Model Results

Forebay Elevations

Before comparing modeled outflow temperatures, it is helpful to compare the modeled forebay elevations in each of the operational scenarios, as the timing of the fill schedule can contribute greatly to the resulting temperature regime in the lake. The *biop* operational scenarios generally led to modeled lake levels that closely match the USACE fill curve during spring and early summer. As the summer progressed into the low-flow months, however, minimum flow requirements typically led to outflows exceeding inflows and a gradual decrease in lake level during mid-July through mid-October (fig. 4).

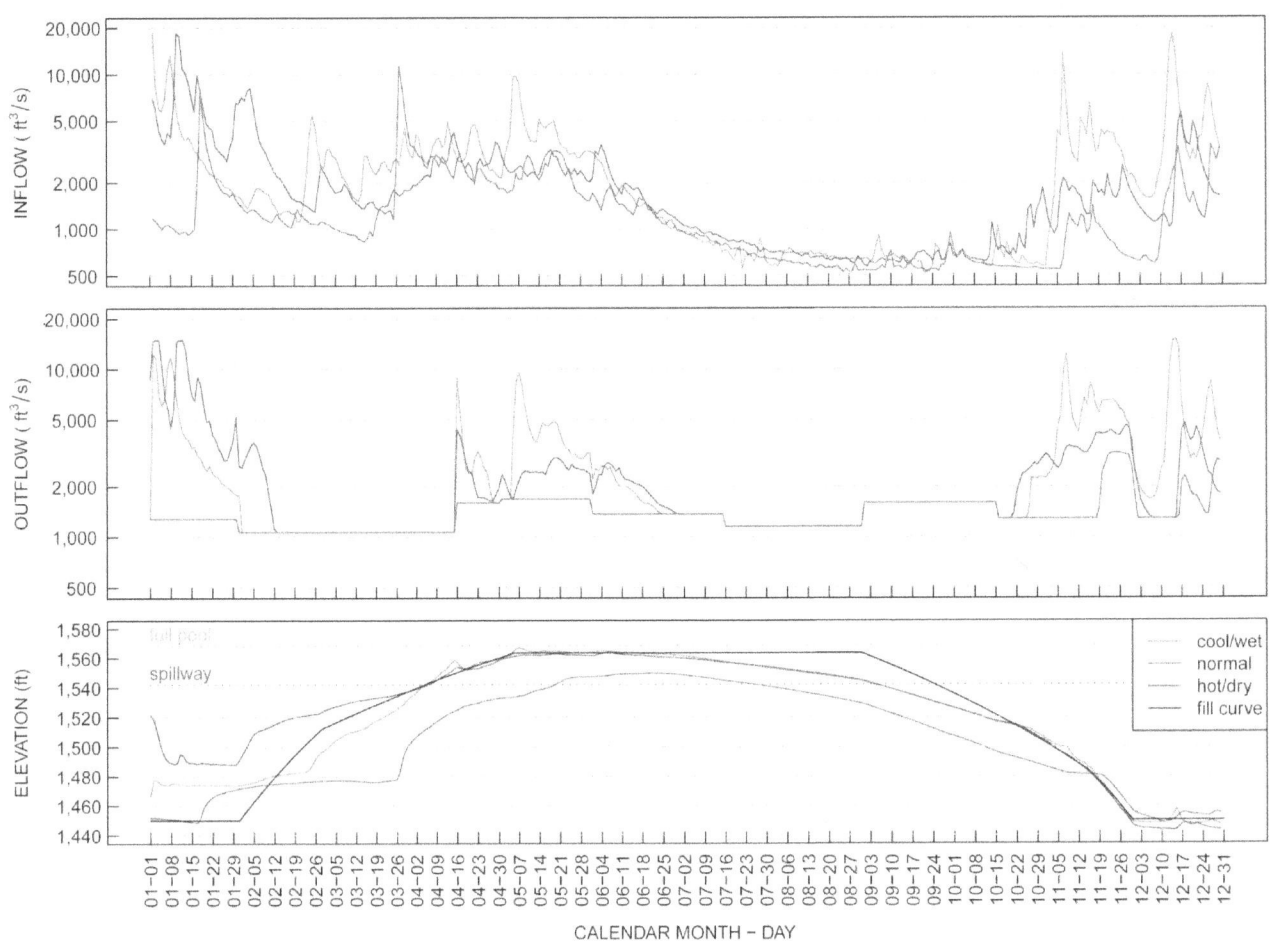

Figure 4. Inflows, computed outflows, and modeled elevation comparison for *biop* operational scenarios.

When minimum outflows are decreased in summer under operational scenario *spill_ext* (table 3), the lake remains closer to full until the fill curve dictates that the lake be drafted down to make room for potential flood storage. In this scenario, drawdown typically began in mid- to late September (fig. 5).

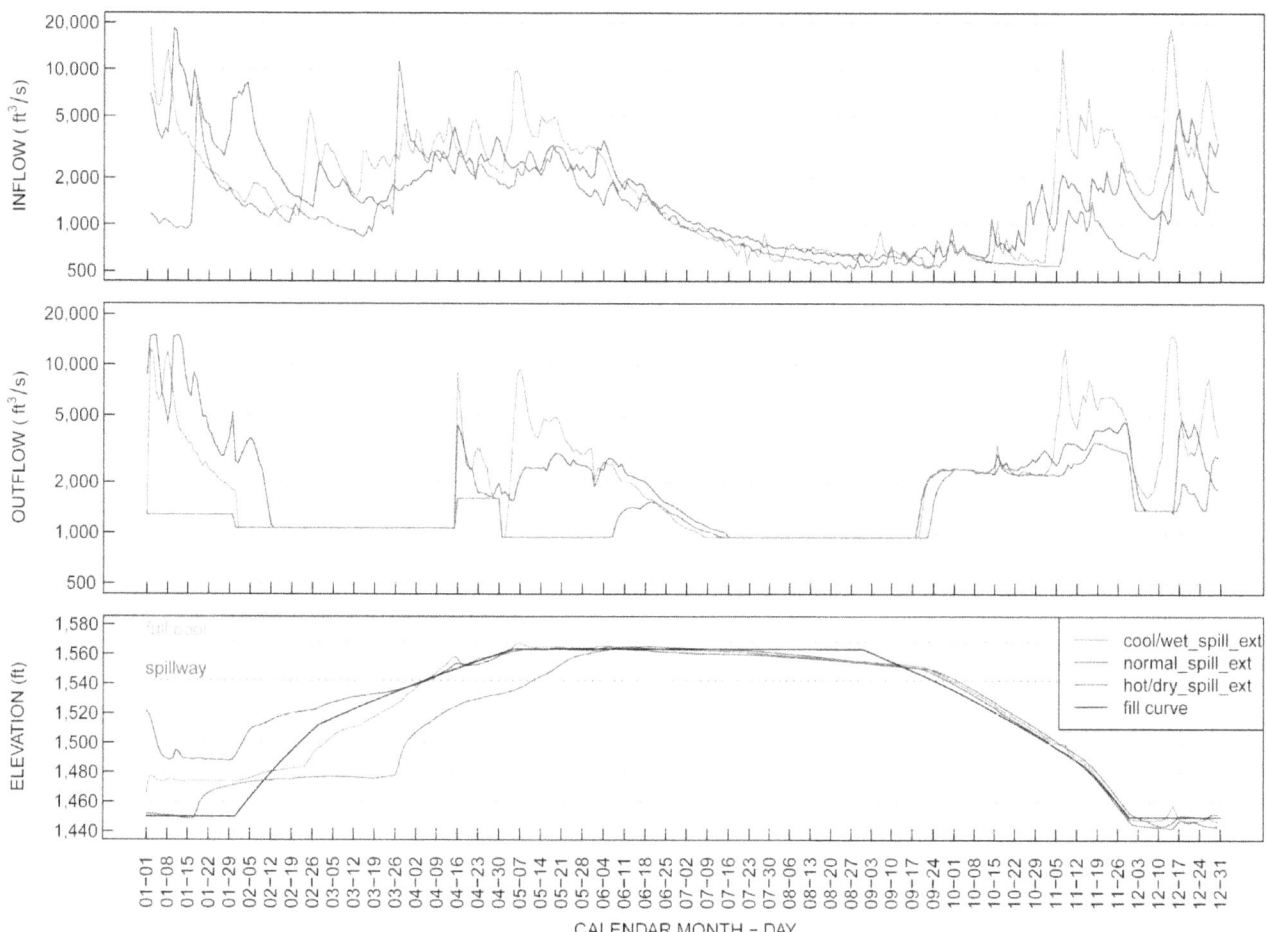

Figure 5. Inflows, computed outflows, and modeled elevation comparison for *spill_ext* operational scenarios.

By extending the time in which the lake remains at or closer to full pool, as in operational scenario *spill_ext30*, forebay elevations remain above the spillway crest generally until mid-October (fig. 6). Also noticeable in this scenario is the steeper drawdown that occurs during autumn compared to that specified by the fill curve.

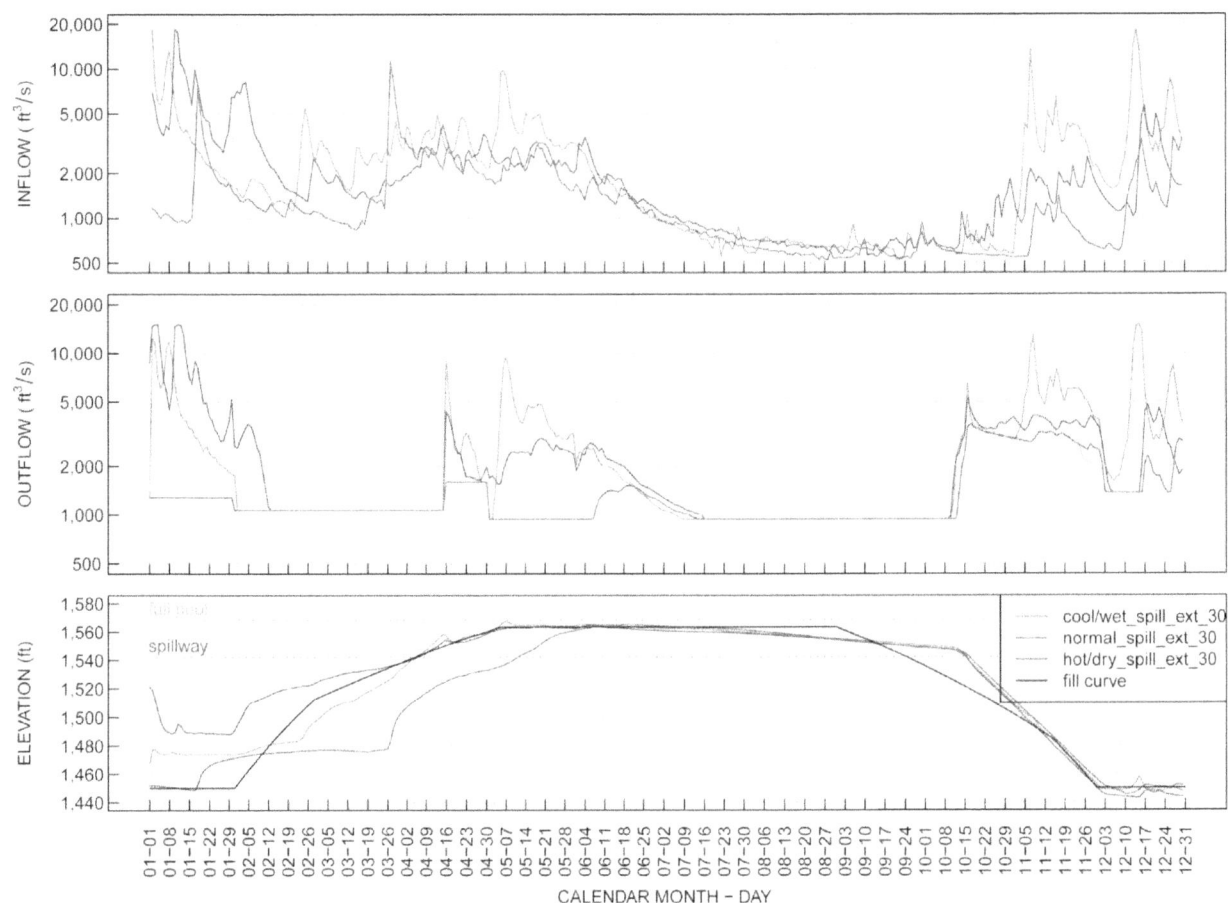

Figure 6. Inflows, computed outflows, and modeled elevation comparison for *spill_ext30* operational scenarios.

A further extension of the time in which Detroit Lake remains at or close to full pool, for roughly 45 days later than specified by the existing USACE fill curve, is used to create the operational scenario *spill_ext45* (fig. 7). This scenario results in sustained forebay elevations above the spillway generally until the beginning of November as well as a 15-day delay of when the minimum conservation pool is reached compared to the existing USACE fill curve. Each of these operational scenarios has ramifications for the availability of the spillway as a means of releasing near-surface water, as well as the release temperatures that can be achieved.

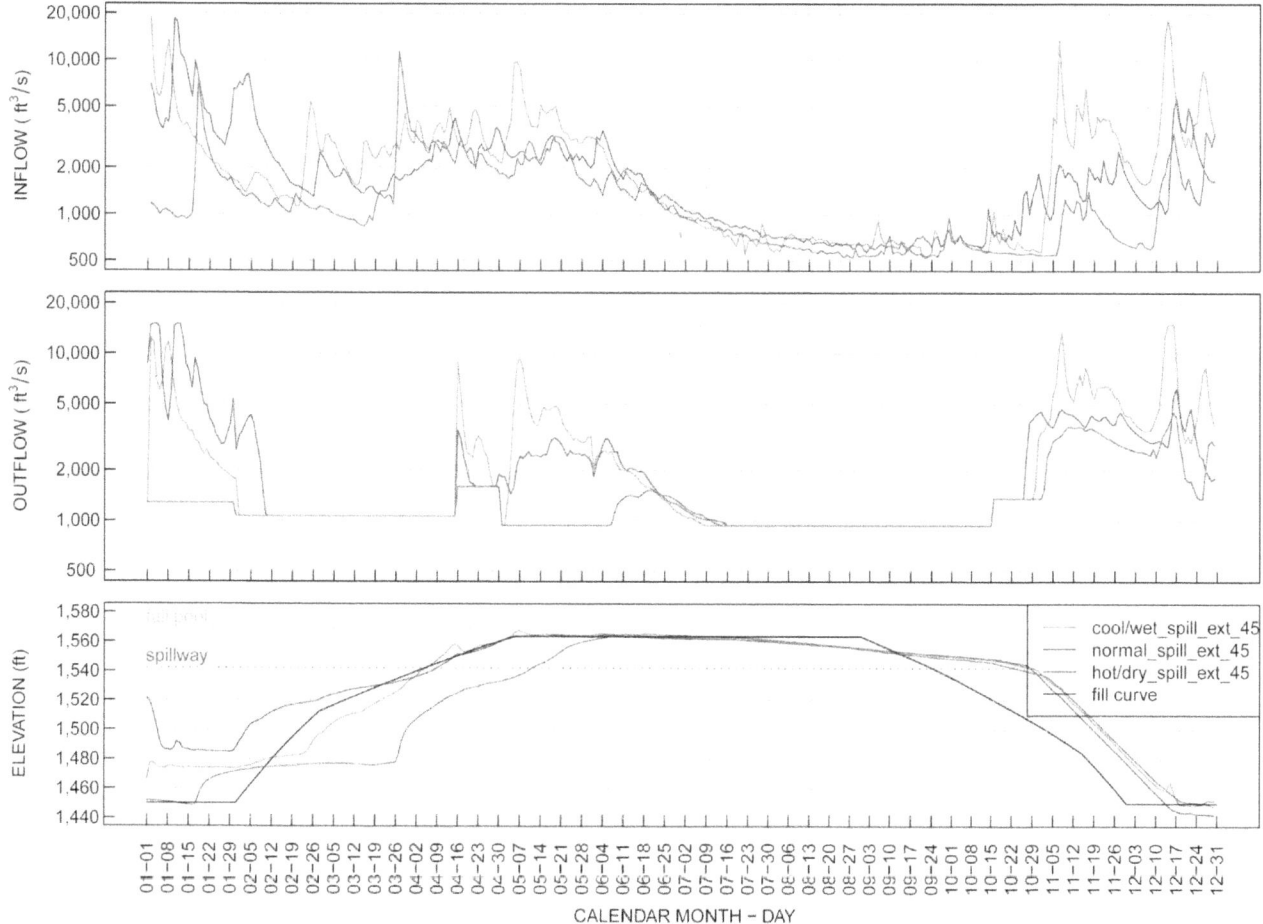

Figure 7. Inflows, computed outflows, and modeled elevation comparison for *spill_ext45* operational scenarios.

Release Water Temperatures

Modeled temperatures from the *existing* structural scenarios serve as a baseline to compare other structural and operational scenario outcomes. Whether the minimum or maximum temperature target was used throughout the summer generally determined the magnitude and timing of the increase in the released water temperature that occurred later in autumn (figs. 8 and 9). Both the minimum and maximum temperature target are plotted in figures 8 through 15,

but only the specified *min* or *max* was used to drive the blending algorithm within CE-QUAL-W2. In the following figures, percent spill is defined as the percentage of total flow that was directed to outlets other than the power penstocks. A minimum of 40 percent of the total release rate was directed to the power penstocks in the *existing* scenarios to allow a minimum amount of power generation.

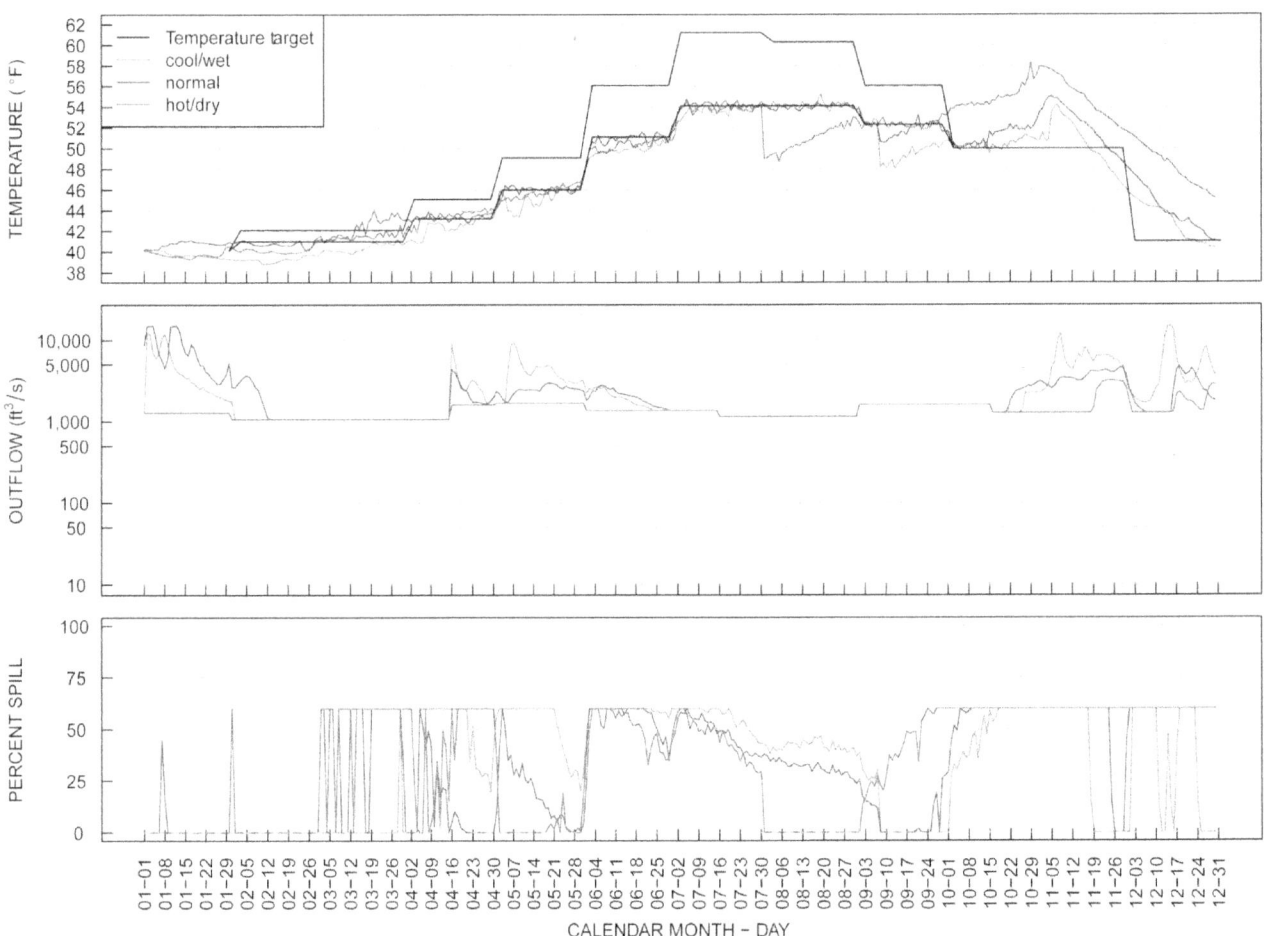

Figure 8. Modeled water temperature, outflow discharge, and percent spill for *existing* structural scenarios with *biop* operational scenarios, and *min* temperature targets (scenarios *cmin1, nmin1, hmin1*) .

16

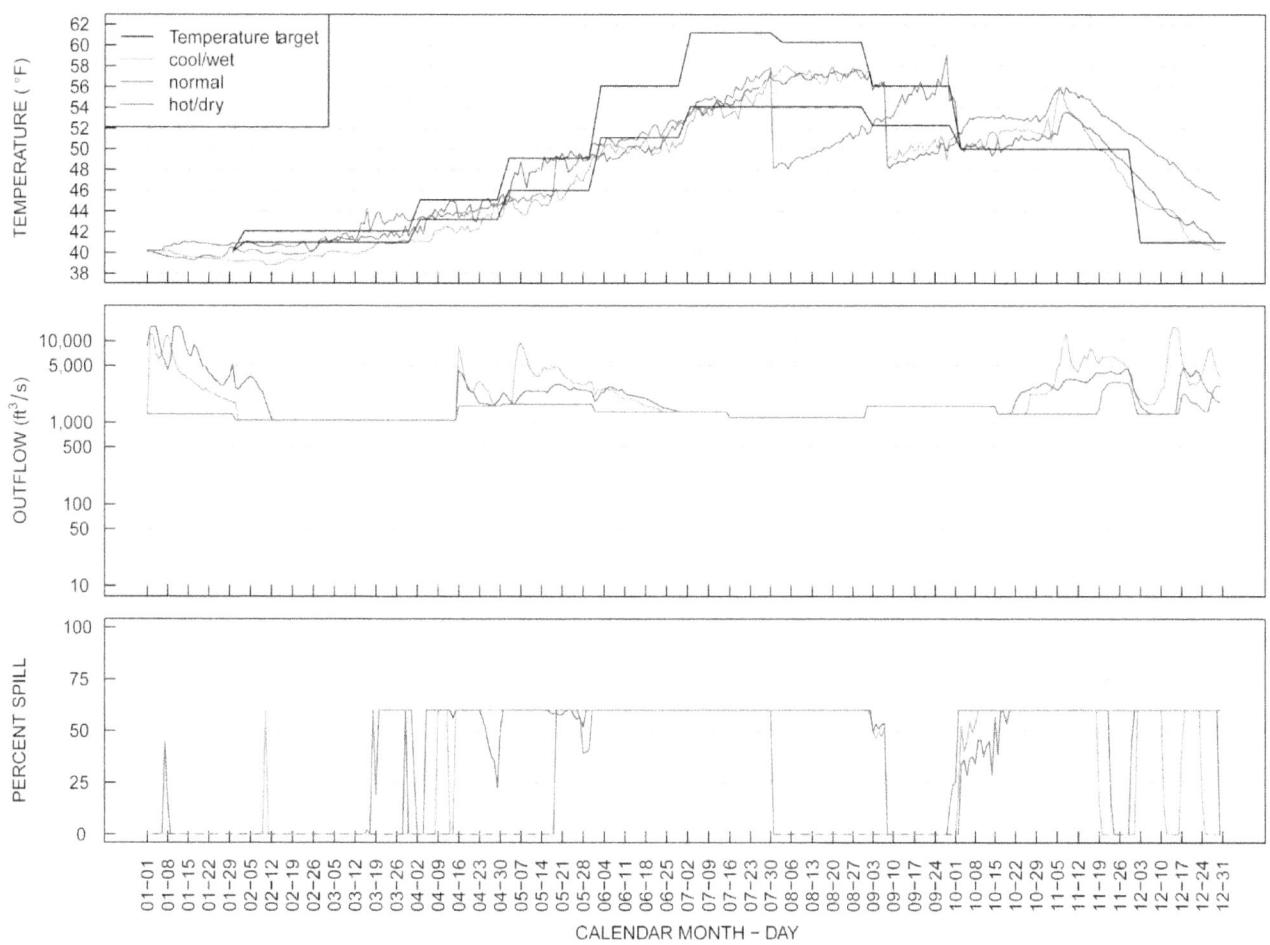

Figure 9. Modeled water temperature, outflow discharge, and percent spill for *existing* structural scenarios with *biop* operational scenarios, and *max* temperature targets (scenarios *cmax1, nmax1, hmax1*).

When the minimum flow releases are decreased and dam operations are adjusted to allow for spillway use later in the year (operational scenario spill_ext_45), temperature management in autumn is generally more successful. During October and November, results from the *min* temperature target scenarios showed that outflow temperatures generally did not exceed the temperature targets by more than 4 °F (fig. 10) wheras the *max* temperature target scenarios did not exceed the temperature targets by more than 2 °F (fig. 11).

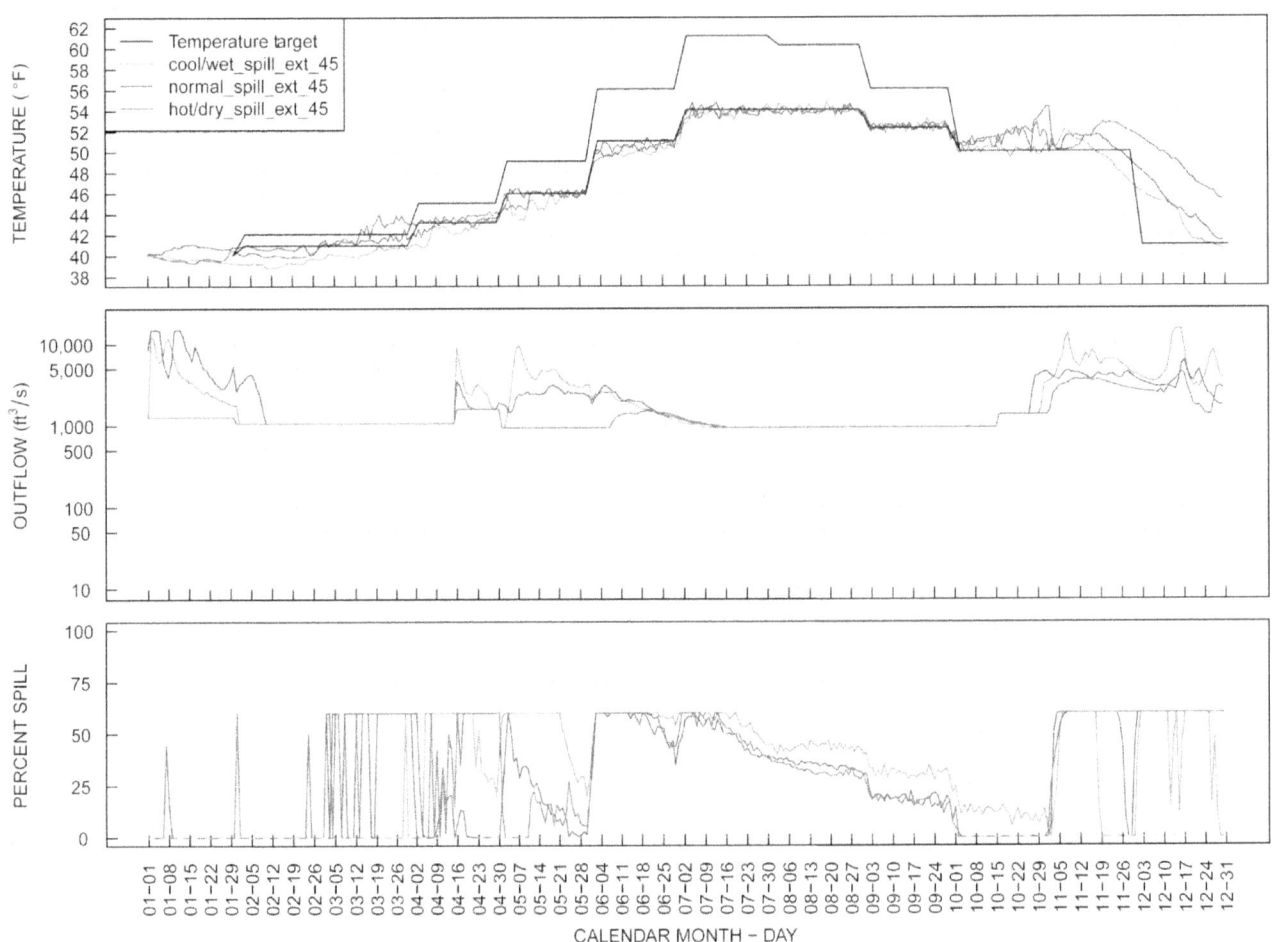

Figure 10. Modeled water temperature, outflow discharge, and percent spill for *existing* structural scenarios with *spill_ext_45* operational scenarios, and *min* temperature targets (scenarios *cmin4, nmin4, hmin4*).

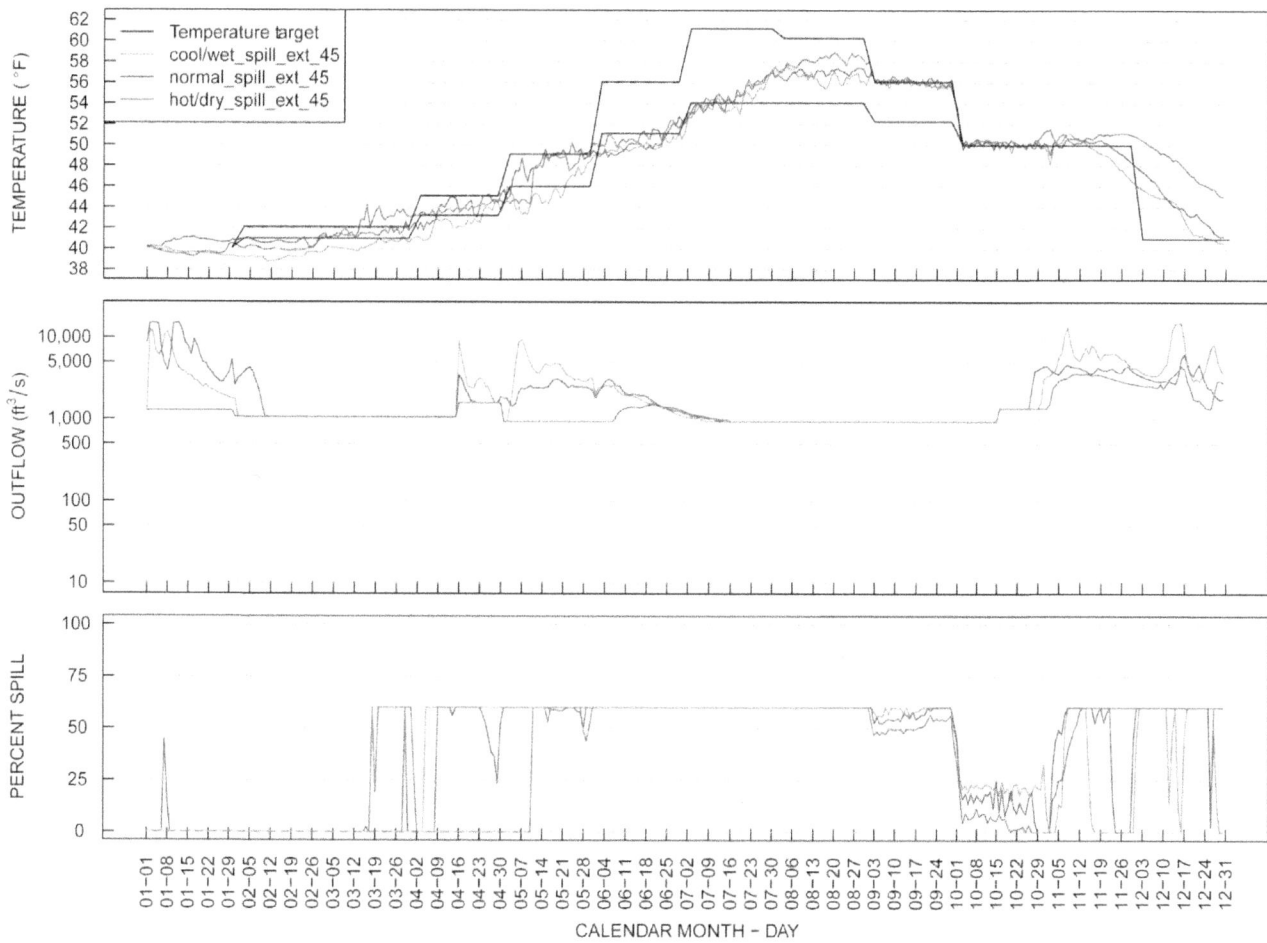

Figure 11. Modeled water temperature, outflow discharge, and percent spill for existing structural scenarios with *spill_ext_45* operational scenarios, and *max* temperature targets (scenarios *cmax4, nmax4, hmax4*).

Structural scenarios in which a single sliding-gate outlet was used led to modeled outflow temperatures that generally varied more from day to day compared to releases using *existing* structural scenarios (figs. 12 and 13). This tendency was especially evident in autumn. The large variation in the release temperatures is a result of the sliding-gate outlet being positioned at a depth that often is located in the middle of the thermocline, such that any seiching of the lake causes the thermocline to move up and down over the course of the day and thereby change the temperature of the water that goes into the outlet. The model scenario was set up so that the elevation of the sliding-gate outlet was adjusted by the model only once per day. Temperature targets were met for most of the year under *slider1340* scenarios, with the exception of scenarios *nmin5* and *hmin5* in which the temperature targets were exceeded in the fall (fig. 12).

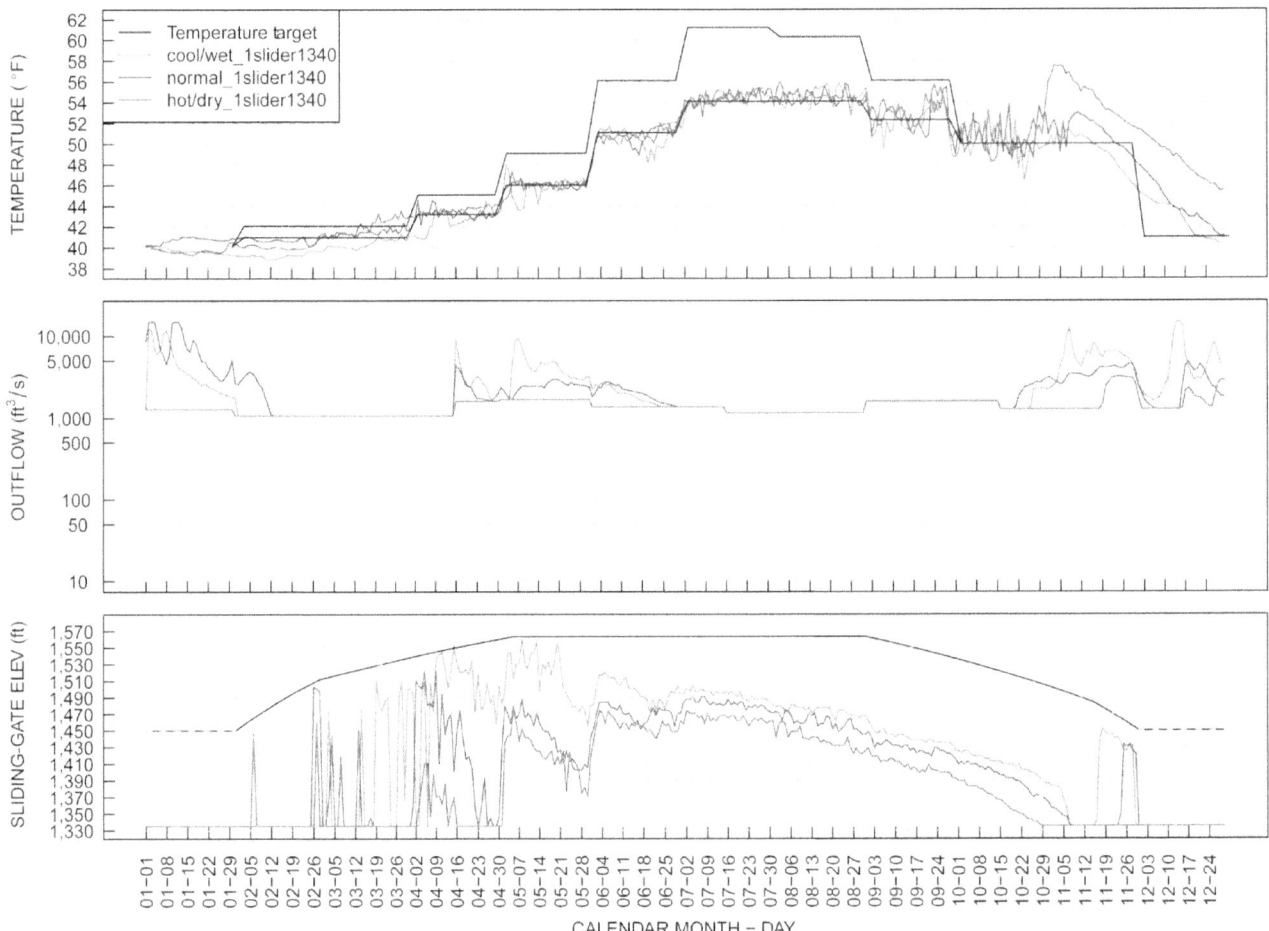

Figure 12. Modeled water temperature, sliding-gate outlet discharge, and sliding-gate outlet elevation for *slider1340* structural scenarios with *biop* operational scenarios, and *min* temperature targets (scenarios *cmin5, nmin5, hmin5*).

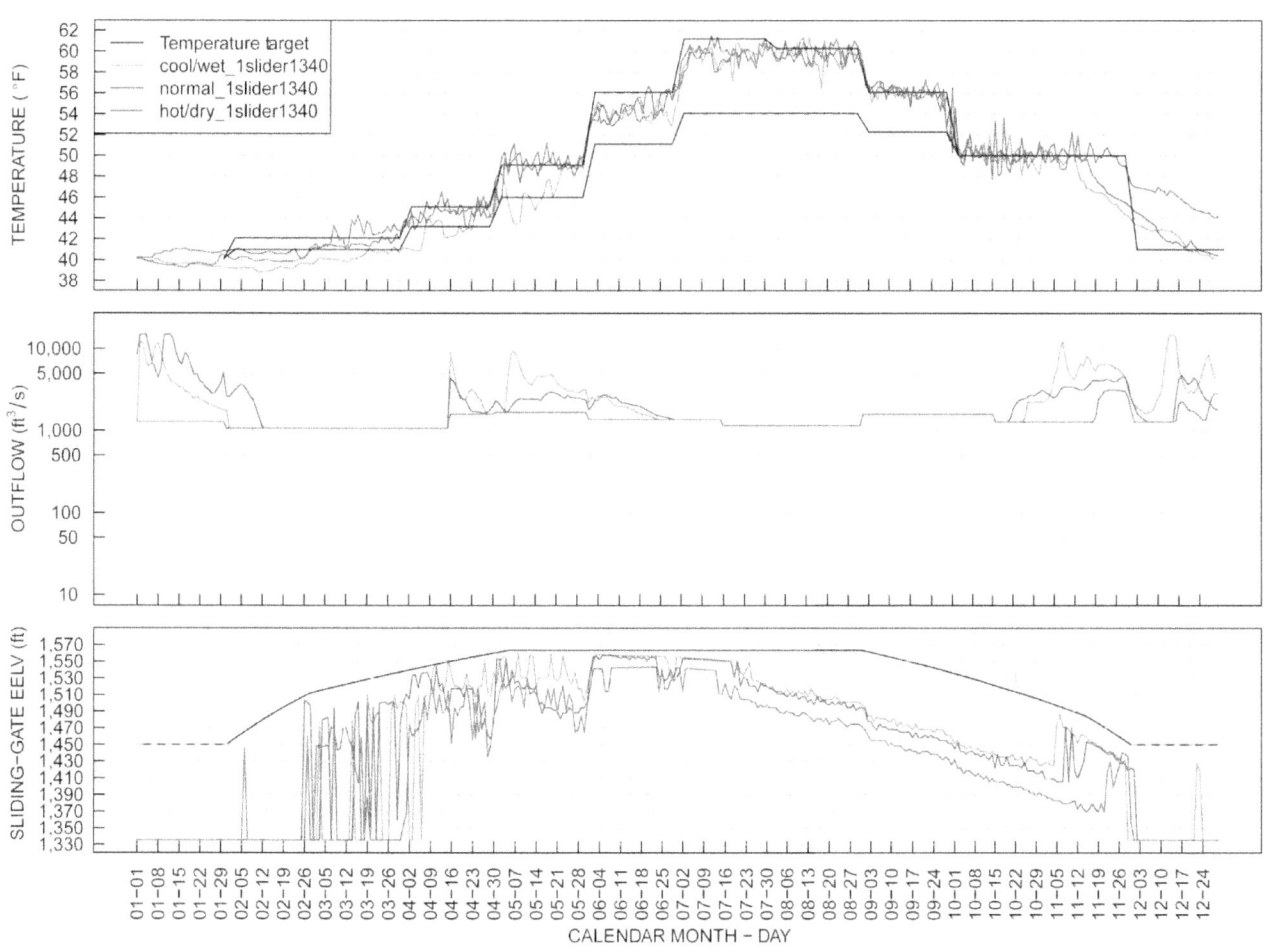

Figure 13. Modeled water temperature, sliding-gate outlet discharge, and sliding-gate outlet elevation for *slider1340* structural scenarios with *biop* operational scenarios, and *max* temperature targets (scenarios *cmax5, nmax5, hmax5*).

Structural scenarios in which a fixed-elevation outlet and a floating outlet were used in combination (*1340floater*) led to modeled release temperatures that are similar to results from the *slider1340* scenarios, but generally contained far less daily variation (figs. 14 and 15). Similar to *nmin5* and *hmin5* above, *nmin6* and *hmin6* release temperatures exceeded the temperature target in the autumn (fig. 14).

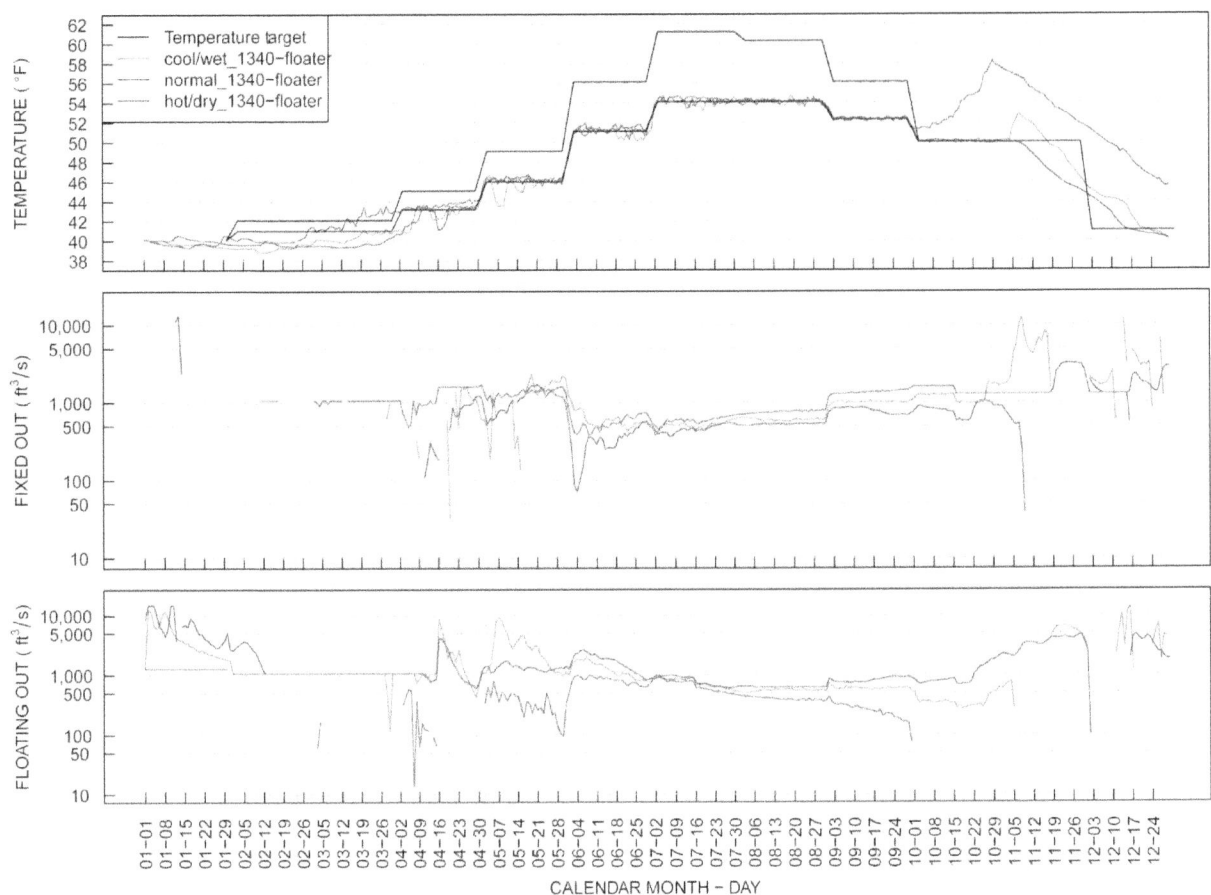

Figure 14. Modeled water temperature, fixed-elevation outlet discharge, and floating outlet discharge for *1340floater* structural scenarios with *biop* operational scenarios, and *min* temperature targets (scenarios *cmin6*, *nmin6*, *hmin6*).

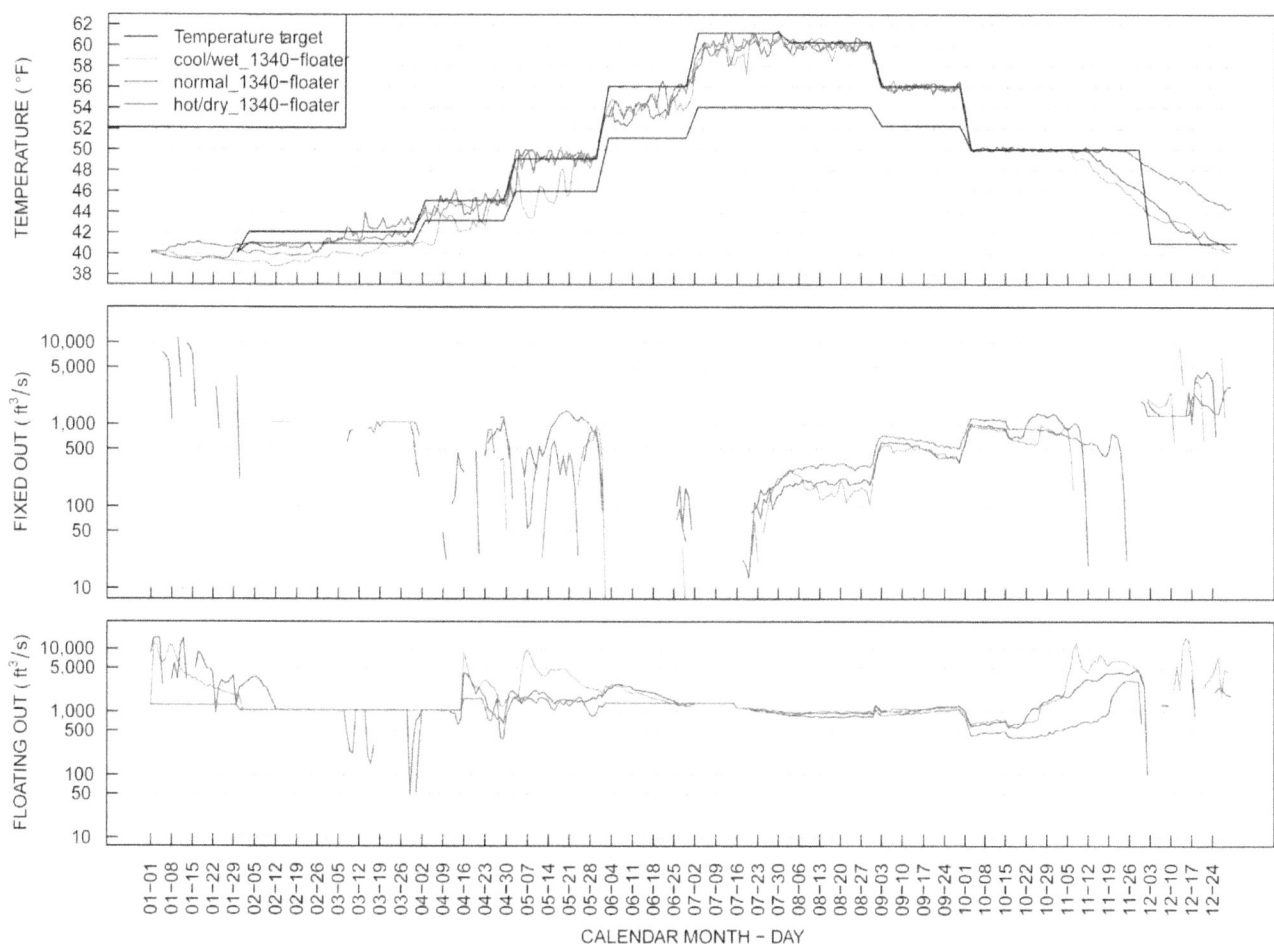

Figure 15. Modeled water temperature, fixed-elevation outlet discharge, and floating outlet discharge for *1340floater* structural scenarios with *biop* operational scenarios, and *max* temperature targets (scenarios *cmax6, nmax6, hmax6*).

Discussion and Conclusions

The Detroit Dam model results show the range of release temperatures that might occur under varying hydrologic and meteorological conditions as well as under several operational and structural scenarios. A common theme among all model results is that spring and summer dam operations tend to determine the flexibility and control of release temperatures that are possible later in autumn. Model results indicate that as early in the year as April, solar radiation heats the surface of the lake and thermal stratification begins. Because most of the lake profile is still relatively cool at that time, the ability to meet downstream temperature targets during spring is dependent on an ability to access and release warmer water near the lake surface. This can be difficult to do when the lake surface is either well below or above the spillway crest in spring and early summer. As the surface of the lake becomes warmer throughout the summer, access to cool water below the thermocline begins to decrease from about June until about mid-November, at which point the lake has been drawn down to make room for flood storage and autumn inflows lead to an isothermal lake profile. In general, the release of warm surface water from the lake during summer allows the cooler water deeper in the lake to be saved until autumn when that cold water is needed most to meet downstream temperature targets.

The ability to mix and release (warm) lake surface water with (cold) deeper water throughout the year often is the limiting factor in controlling release temperatures from Detroit Lake. The existing outlets at Detroit Dam do not allow near-surface waters to be released during times when the lake elevation is below the spillway crest (spring and autumn). During years in which the reservoir may be late to fill or not fill at all (as seen in *hot/dry* and *biop* model scenarios), the spillway may only be a viable release point for a limited time in summer. Immediately after the lake is drawn down below the spillway crest elevation, dam operations must withdraw cool water

from below the thermocline by using the power penstock gates. Later in the year, the cool water supply below the thermocline can become exhausted at the elevation of the available outlets and an uncontrollable rise in release temperatures typically results from about October through November. Thus, the existing structure restricts the managers and operators of Detroit Dam to blending for only a portion of the year with even less flexibility in drier years.

Model simulations indicate that by delaying the drawdown of Detroit Lake in autumn, better control over release temperatures is possible. This is mostly the result of the extended use of the spillway until as late as November 1 (*spill_ext_45* scenarios in fig. 7). This allows warm epilimnetic water to be released and blended with cool water from the hypolimnion, thereby rationing the deeper cool-water supply throughout the autumn. As a result of this sustained use of the spillway under *spill_ext_45* operational scenarios (figs. 10 and 11), the abrupt change in release temperature caused by the loss of spillway usage in autumn is not as apparent as with *biop* operational scenarios (figs. 8 and 9). Whether this abrupt change in release temperatures occurs may be a consideration for downstream salmon habitat during late summer and autumn.

Aside from operationally delaying the drawdown of Detroit Lake, a number of simulated structural scenarios have shown that floating or sliding-gate outlets can provide greater control over outflow temperatures than the existing outlets at Detroit Dam. While release temperatures from both the *slider1340* and *1340floater* structural scenarios were able to roughly meet the *max* temperature targets (figs. 13 and 15), the latter showed far less day to day temperature variation than the former. This illustrates the value provided by having two outlets to access warm and cold water separately throughout the year. As the thermocline moves up and down in the water column on a monthly and daily basis, a more variable release temperature results from a single sliding-gate outlet (*slider1340*) than from a blended combination of one floating outlet withdrawing warmer surface water and one fixed-elevation outlet at a given depth withdrawing cooler water (*1340floater*).

Although structural scenarios involving sliding-gate and floating outlets resulted in release temperatures that met *max* temperature targets, some *min* temperature target scenarios led to release temperatures in exceedance of these targets during autumn. All *hot/dry* structural scenarios (*existing, slider1340,* and *1340floater*) exceeded *min* temperature targets in autumn. Meeting the minimum temperature target in the autumn of *hot/dry* conditions may require structural scenarios that have the ability to withdraw water from deeper in the lake, below the elevation of 1,340 ft. On the other hand, it is likely that *min* temperature targets would not be used during midsummer of a particularly hot year.

Model results show that the ability to control release temperatures and meet downstream temperature targets throughout the year can be more closely attained at Detroit Dam by either delaying drawdown of the lake in autumn or by installing a well-conceived combination of floating and/or sliding-gate outlets. Integration of these results with the additional downstream temperature models of Big Cliff Reservoir and the North Santiam River will occur later in this study and will be incorporated into a USGS Scientific Investigations Report to be published in 2012. That final report will supersede the interim results presented in this report.

References Cited

Cole, T.M., and Wells, S.A., 2002, CE-QUAL-W2: A two-dimensional, laterally averaged, hydrodynamic and water-quality model, version 3.1: U.S. Army Corps of Engineers, Instruction Report EL-02-1 [variously paged].

National Marine Fisheries Service, 2008, Willamette Basin Biological Opinion—Endangered Species Act Section 7(a)(2) Consultation: NOAA Fisheries Log Number F/NWR/2000/02117 [variously paged], accessed October 20, 2009, at *http://www.nwr.noaa.gov/Salmon-Hydropower/Willamette-Basin/Willamette-BO.cfm.*

Rounds, S.A. and Sullivan, A.B., 2006, Development and use of new routines in CE-QUAL-W2 to blend water from multiple reservoir outlets to meet downstream temperature targets, in Proceedings of the Third Federal Interagency Hydrologic Modeling Conference, April 2-6, 2006, Reno, NV: Subcommittee on Hydrology of the Interagency Advisory Committee on Water Information, ISBN 0-9779007-0-3. (Also available at *http://or.water.usgs.gov/tualatin/fihmc3_w2_modifications.pdf.*)

Sullivan, A.B. and Rounds, S.A., 2006, Modeling water-quality effects of structural and operational changes to Scoggins Dam and Henry Hagg Lake, Oregon: U.S. Geological Survey Scientific Investigations Report 2006-5060, 36 p. (Also available at *http://pubs.usgs.gov/sir/2006/5060/.*)

Sullivan, A.B., Rounds, S.A., Sobieszczyk, S., and Bragg, H.M., 2007, Modeling hydrodynamics, water temperature, and suspended sediment in Detroit Lake, Oregon: U.S. Geological Survey Scientific Investigations Report 2007-5008, 40 p. (Also available at *http://pubs.usgs.gov/sir/2007/5008/.*)

Appendix A

This appendix includes graphs showing results from the balance of the model scenarios. They were excluded from the main body of the report because of their similarity to the others.

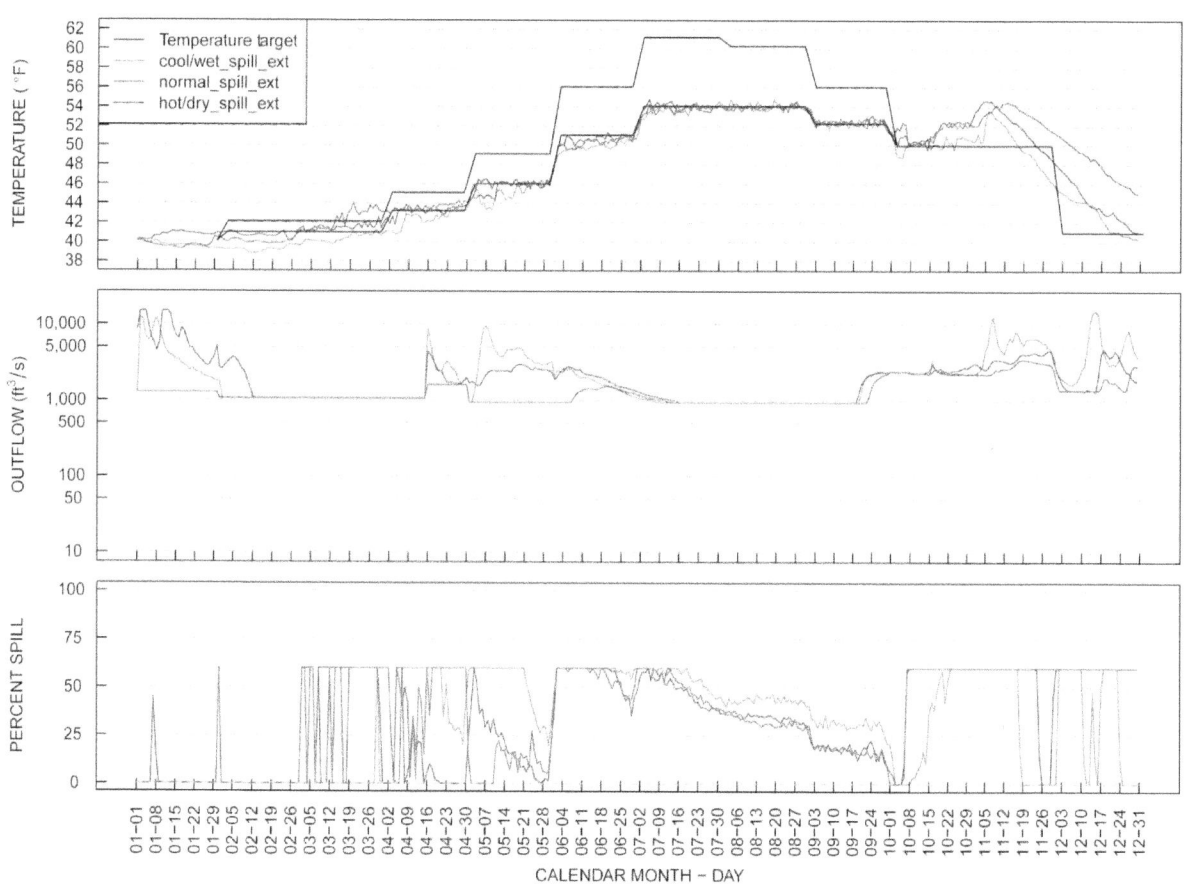

Figure A1. Modeled water temperature, outflow discharge, and percent spill for *existing* structural scenarios with *spill_ext* operational scenarios, and *min* temperature targets (scenarios *cmin2, nmin2, hmin2*).

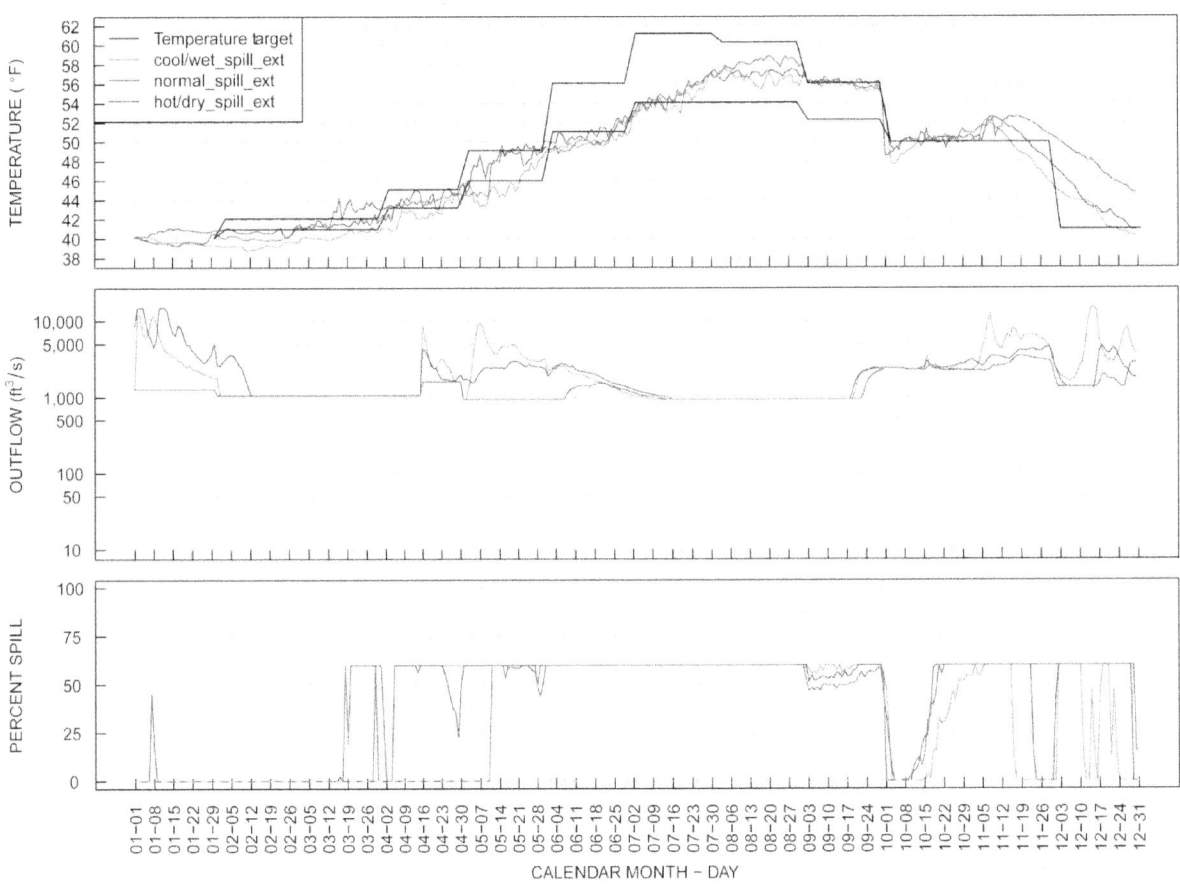

Figure A2. Modeled water temperature, outflow discharge, and percent spill for *existing* structural scenarios with *spill_ext* operational scenarios, and *max* temperature targets (scenarios *cmax2, nmax2, hmax2*).

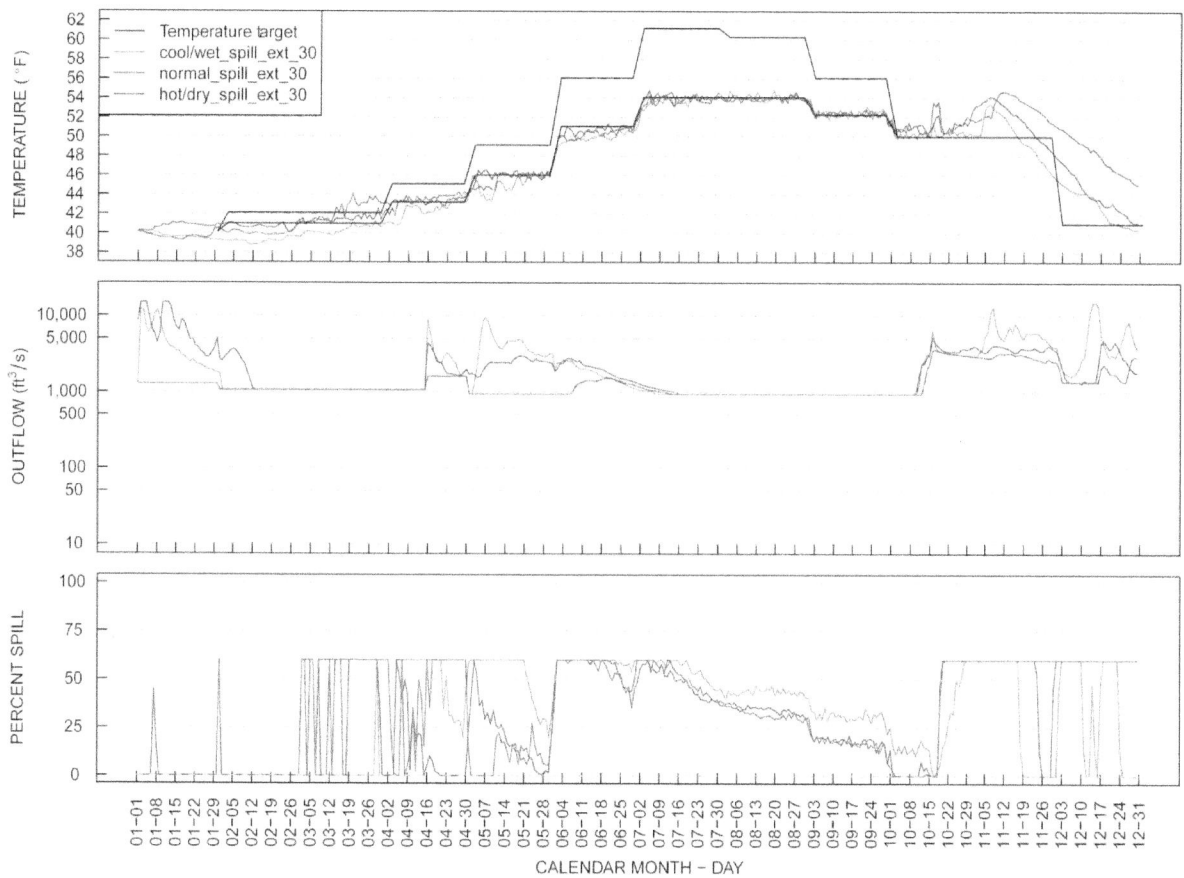

Figure A3. Modeled water temperature, outflow discharge, and percent spill for *existing* structural scenarios with *spill_ext_30* operational scenarios, and *min* temperature targets (scenarios *cmin3, nmin3, hmin3*).

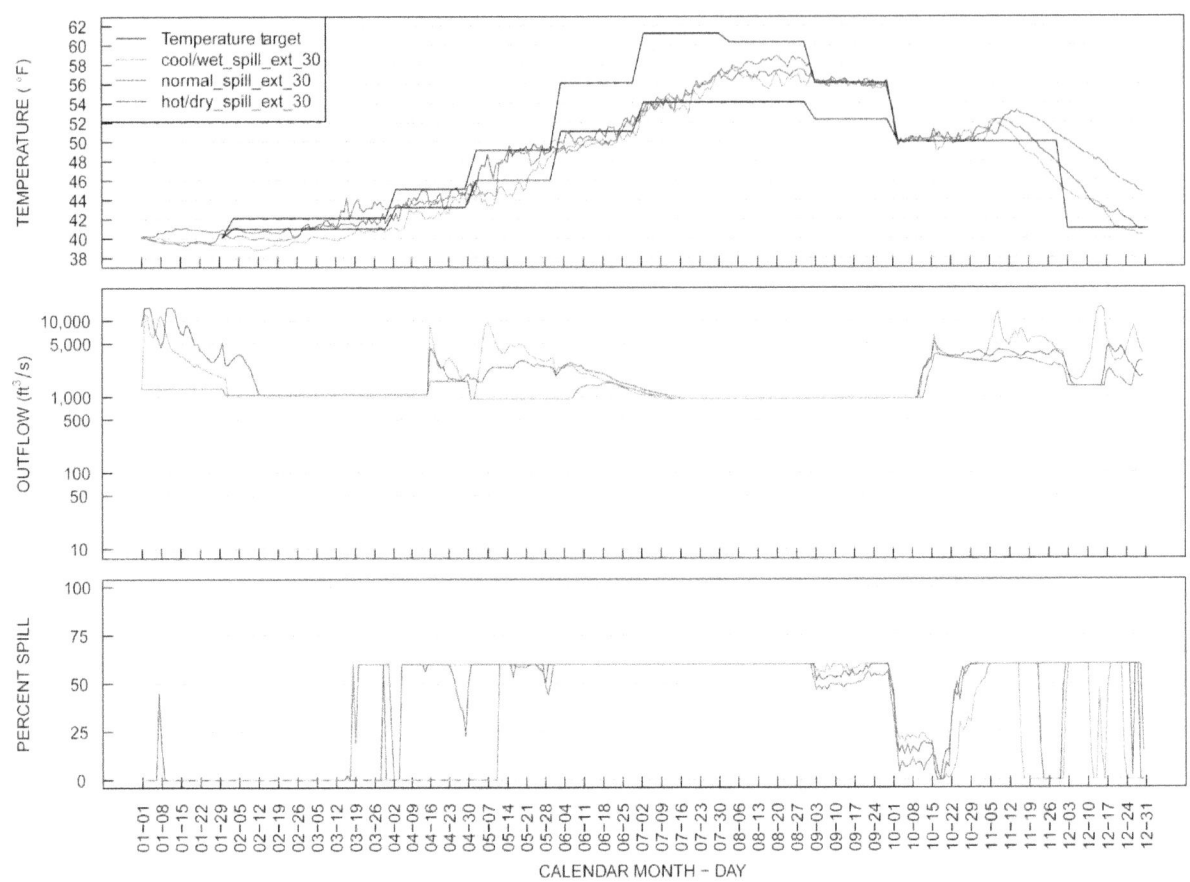

Figure A4. Modeled water temperature, outflow discharge, and percent spill for *existing* structural scenarios with *spill_ext_30* operational scenarios, and *max* temperature targets (scenarios *cmax3, nmax3, hmax3*).

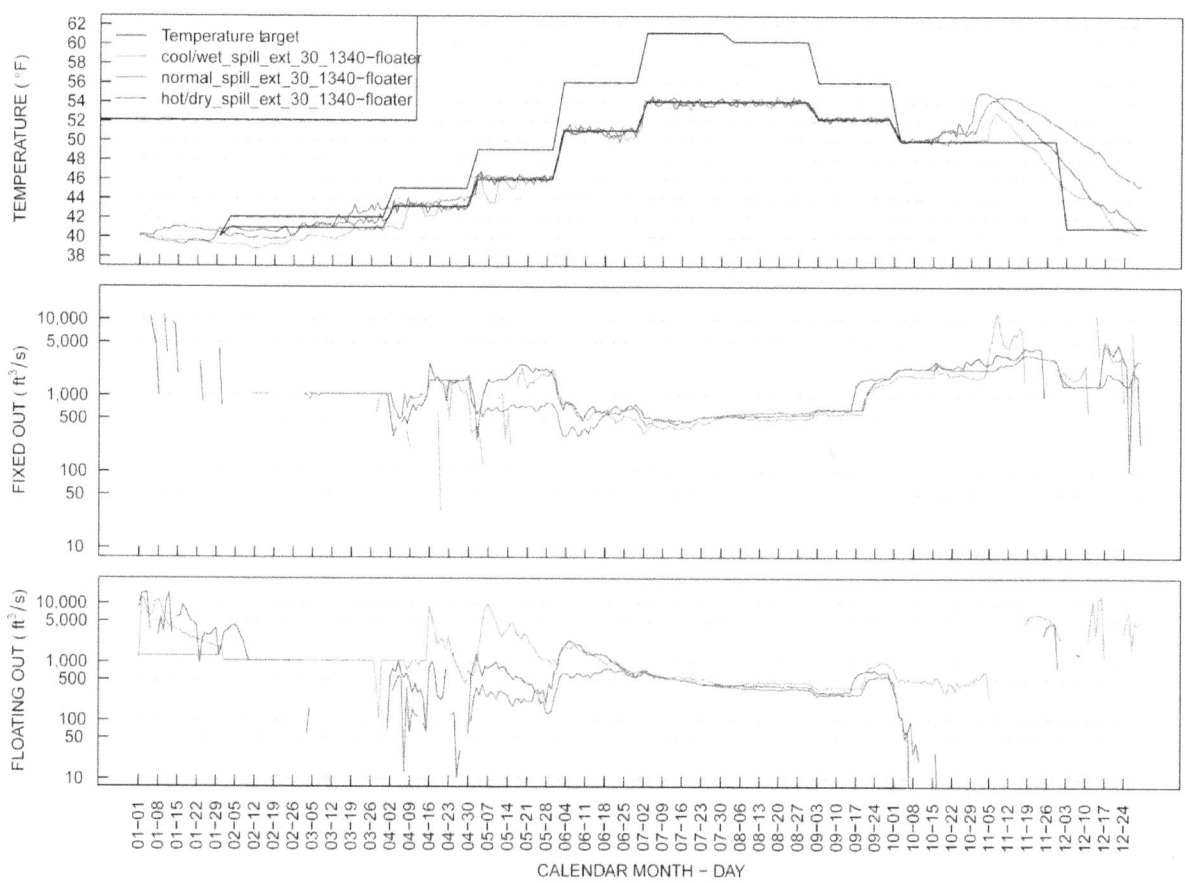

Figure A5. Modeled water temperature, fixed-elevation outlet discharge, and floating outlet discharge for *1340floater* structural scenarios with *spill_ext_30* operational scenarios, and *min* temperature targets (scenarios *cmin7, nmin7, hmin7*).

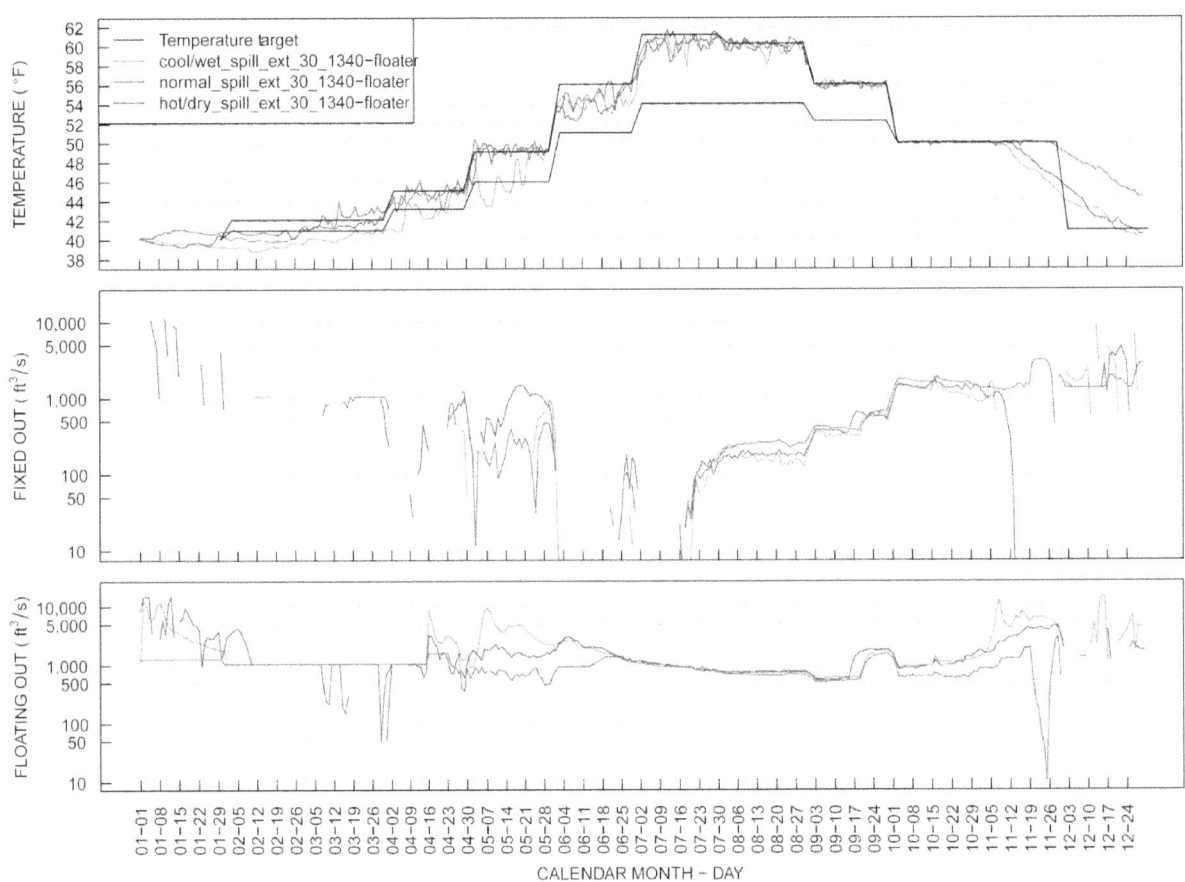

Figure A6. Modeled water temperature, fixed-elevation outlet discharge, and floating outlet discharge for *1340floater* structural scenarios with *spill_ext_30* operational scenarios, and *max* temperature targets (scenarios *cmax7, nmax7, hmax7*).